Bible studies on Genesis 1–11

Mark Vander Hart

Reformed Fellowship, Inc.
3363 Hickory Ridge Ct. SW
Grandville, MI 49418

Printed in the United States of America

For information:
Reformed Fellowship, Inc.
3363 Hickory Ridge Ct. SW
Grandville, MI 49418
Phone: 616.532.8510
Web: reformedfellowship.net
Email: sales@reformedfellowship.net

Book design by Jeff Steenholdt

ISBN 978-0-9653981-7-6

Contents

Preface

There may be some who wonder whether another work that examines Genesis 1–11 is necessary. After all, have there not been enough books, articles, and studies produced already? It is true that much has been written on the opening chapters of Genesis, some of it very valuable, and some of it not so valuable.

These Bible study lessons were prepared at the request of the Board of Reformed Fellowship, and they originally appeared in *The Outlook* magazine, the monthly publication of Reformed Fellowship. Over the years Reformed Fellowship has been very interested in producing Bible study materials so that God's people may increase their understanding of what God's Word, the Bible, says. No one has to be told to be ignorant; we can do that on our own! Instead, we need to encourage the study of and meditation on God's Word. But even more, we need to apply to our faith and practice, all that God has said to us.

These lessons were prepared, not to repeat the many things that have been said before, but to review what we know and to think again about material in the Bible we do not know (or do not know that well). These lessons were produced with several firm convictions. First, when Moses wrote by inspiration what we call Genesis 1–11, he was already writing about Christ (see John 5:46). Second, Genesis 1–11 clearly reveals the reality of God's kingdom, i.e., His sovereign rule over everything, a rule in grace and judgment. Third, God carries out this sovereign rule historically in the manner of a covenant, a life relationship with those whom God chooses for His good pleasure. Christ, the kingdom of God, and His covenant—these are basic to the Bible and in evidence from the start. The reader will see this worked out in the various lessons.

This is a Bible study. Therefore, it is my hope and prayer that you, the reader, will give yourself adequate time to read through each lesson, but even more importantly, to check out the other Bible references. Comparing Scripture with Scripture is a hallmark of a Reformed study of Scripture.

The Bible versions that I have used are the New International Version (NIV) and the New American Standard Bible (NASB). In addition to the text of Scripture itself, I also direct you to the Reformed confessions, to the Three Forms of Unity and the Westminster Standards. Please make use of these documents as well to increase your appreciation of how Reformed and Presbyterian churches have confessed the precious truths revealed on the pages of Holy Writ. May your study of Genesis 1–11 lead you to sing with the psalmist, "I rejoice at Thy word like one who finds great spoil" (Ps. 119:162).

Rev. Mark Vander Hart
July, 1999

Lesson 1

Story or History?

Read Genesis 1:1–2:3; II Timothy 3

Our Lord Jesus Christ once asked His disciples whether they understood the parables that He had spoken (Matt. 13). They said that they did. To which our Lord replied, "Therefore every scribe who has become a disciple of the kingdom of heaven is like a head of a household, who brings forth out of his treasure things new and old" (Matt. 13:52).

Engaging in a study of Genesis 1–11 will be for us, I should hope, an exercise that will remind us of things that are "old" and well-known, but also an exercise that will inform us and challenge us in "new" things as well. Studying areas of the Bible that have been frequently covered is risky in the sense that we may think we know all of it quite well. In such a case, we are not always open to learning the things that God has placed in His Word. One can and should always learn something new when he or she opens up the Bible again to read it and to listen to His message again in childlike faith.

Some Bible study basics: the Author and the author

The Christian confesses certain things about God's Word, the Bible. In II Peter 1:20–21 (NASB) we read the following:

"But know this first of all, that no prophecy of Scripture is a matter of one's own interpretation, for no prophecy was ever made by an act of human will, but men moved by the Holy Spirit spoke from God."

While we would admit that the human authorship of Genesis is not explicitly stated for us, yet this book of beginnings is so integral to the whole of the first five books, the Pentateuch ("five-scrolled"), that we may discuss the human authorship of the whole as inclusive of a discussion concerning the human writer of Genesis. We believe that the man "moved by the Holy Spirit" to write the Pentateuch (and thus Genesis, of course) was the great Old Testament prophet Moses. Support for this comes from the testimony of the Pentateuch itself. Consider the following passages:

Exodus 24:4–8, "And Moses wrote . . ."
Exodus 34:27, ". . . to Moses, 'Write these words'"
Numbers 33:1, 2, "And Moses wrote . . ."
Deuteronomy 31:9, 24–26, "And Moses wrote this law . . ."

In Exodus through Deuteronomy Moses is the prominent figure, the one who received the covenant at Mount Sinai, and the one who wrote out the itinerary of Israel as she traveled through the wilderness to the Plains of Moab. Other Old Testament passages support this as well (cf. Josh. 1:7, 8; 8:31; 22:9; I Kings 2:3; II Kings 14:6; 21:8; 22:8; Ezra 6:18; Neh. 13:1; Mal. 4:4).

The testimony of the New Testament also supports the claim that Moses is the principal human writer of the Pentateuch. The Jews of Jesus' day and our Lord Himself had no question regarding the Mosaic authorship of the Pentateuch. Read and reflect upon these passages as indicative of the general New Testament understanding of Moses as author of the Pentateuch (the "Law"): Matthew 8:4; 19:8; Mark 1:44: 10:5; 12:26; Luke 5:14; 16:16, 31; 24:27, 44; John 5:46–47; 7:19. More could be cited, but these will suffice for now. In short, the witness of the Scripture itself is that Moses wrote the Pentateuch and that this is God's Word that addresses us with binding authority.

Furthermore, we confess that all of Scripture is ultimately from the mouth of God, given to prepare God's people to lead useful lives of service in the kingdom of God. The

Apostle Paul tells Timothy that "all Scripture is inspired by God and profitable for teaching, for reproof, for correction, for training in righteousness; that the man of God may be adequate, equipped for every good work" (II Tim. 3:16–17). When Paul penned these words, he had in mind the Old Testament Scripture because the New Testament documents had not yet been collected and universally recognized as God's inspired Word. Genesis 1–11, as part of that inspired, breathed-out-from-God collection, is also profitable and useful to us today for teaching us positive truths, warning us about destructive errors, and building us up in faith and obedience. As you read Genesis 1–11, try to keep in mind this goal: achieving a godly equipping in teaching and correction.

Some Bible study basics: guidelines to interpretation

To acknowledge one's presuppositions about the text of Scripture is not yet to spell out how one approaches this text as a text. How do we read the Bible? Some say that we should be "literal wherever possible." But does this not run the danger of a kind of flat, two-dimensional reading of Scripture? For example, in classic dispensationalism when the Bible says *Israel,* it means Israel (the children of Jacob), but when it says *church,* it means church, and never shall the two be interchanged. Maybe we could be "figurative" or "allegorical wherever possible." But this is not satisfactory either, because the danger is that our understanding of the Bible is subject to all kinds of fanciful and quite arbitrary interpretations. We could treat the Bible and its message as a "wax nose."

The classic description of a Reformed reading of the Bible is exegesis (interpretation) that gives full weight to the redemptive, the historical, the grammatical, and the covenantal context and concerns of the passage. In the history of how the Bible was interpreted this was the "literal" (i.e., according to the letter) or "literary" reading, giving full allowance for the various types of literature (genres) that compose the Bible, whether those types be historical narrative, legal code, poetry, wisdom statements, prophetic sermons, and the like. God has given us His Word in human words, in a variety of life-settings, in several types of literature. Text in context (actually several contexts!): this must be kept in mind as we read.

The following principles should help us all in our reading of Genesis 1–11 (and even the rest of the Bible). First of all, the words in a passage must not be abstracted (lifted out) from the immediate context. This does not mean that a word or several words might not have special weight or great significance. That can (and does) happen. But what a word means, it means in its context. At the same time, we must recognize that words have denotations (basic, core meanings) as well as connotations (derived, extended, even "poetic" meanings). So, we should always think carefully how the writer uses a word in a particular context.

Secondly, verses too must not be abstracted from their context. The actual division of our Bibles into chapters and numbered verses is several centuries old by now, but we must remember that this was not the case when the Bible was first written. For example, the Gospel writer Luke did not write individual verses; he wrote (under inspiration) a carefully researched account of Christ's life and work (cf. Luke 1:1–4), an account that holds together as a whole.

Thirdly, we must take into account the type of literature in which a passage occurs. This is the matter of genre and the kind of interpretation appropriate to the type of literature at hand. For example, you would not interpret a physics textbook as you would interpret a poem by Robert Frost. You would not read the classified section of a newspaper as you would read a play by William Shakespeare. So, too, the poetry of the Psalms allows for a more emotive, suggestive interpretation that would not be as appropriate in, say, historical narrative.

Fourthly, the overall structure and unity of the Bible must be kept in mind. Because the Bible has one Author, who used many human authors over a great period of time, we believe that the overall message of the Bible is unified. Scripture, because it is unified, is therefore able to interpret itself. The great church father Augustine reminds us that the New Testament's message is contained (concealed) within the Old Testament, while the Old Testament's message is revealed more fully in the New. The basics of God's great message of salvation in Jesus Christ are already given in the Old Testament; the New Testament will throw greater light on the truths already spelled out in the Old. The Apostle Paul reminds Timothy that the Holy Scriptures (the Old Testament!) are "able to make you wise for salvation through faith in Christ Jesus" (II Tim. 3:15).

Finally, we may never allow what we discover and know from extra-biblical material to have an authority and an importance that is the same as, perhaps even higher than, the Bible itself. As we have said earlier, the Scripture is quite able to interpret itself. Knowledge gained from extra-biblical studies should never be ignored, for often such information may throw helpful light on the original languages, the culture, the customs, etc., of the times of the Bible, but the message in the end must be the message that Scripture itself teaches.

Genesis 1–11: challenges to reading

Why do we limit our study to these chapters in the book of beginnings? Why not study, say, Genesis 1–9 or Genesis 1–13? There are several reasons why some have in the past (and even still today) made Genesis 11 the end of a significant section of Genesis. At the end of Genesis 11 the genealogy being traced takes us to Abram and Sarai. Abram (later renamed Abraham in Genesis 17) becomes the main figure in the story line that takes us to Genesis 25. The story line focuses on God's covenantal dealings with one man, while in the chapters before Abram there are accounts of worldwide events and long genealogical lists. The history and genealogies recorded in Genesis 1–11 obviously take us back to the very beginning of time, and that has led some to ask the question, "Is this all true as a record? Could the things recorded in Genesis 1–11 really have happened? Or, do we in fact have stories that are really more like myths, sagas, or legends?"

Such a challenge arises out of a variety of sciences which themselves have been developing in the last three hundred or so years. In particular the challenges and questions about how we should read Genesis 1–11 have come from the sciences of physics, geology, paleontology, archaeology, literary analysis, and historiography. A straightforward reading of Genesis 1–11 could lead one to believe that the world was likely created just slightly earlier than 4000 B.C., that it was once inundated by a world–wide flood, and that a godly line of people kept alive religious traditions which in time became inscripturated in the Pentateuch, the first five books of Moses. But some scientists, especially since the time of the Enlightenment (late 17th through the 18th centuries) have come to doubt the Biblical account in terms of its description of actual events in time and space.

What is a responsible, Christian viewpoint toward this? Does Genesis 1–11 record *history* (facts that describe real people and places, in actual time and space), or do we have here merely *stories* whose value lies in the "ideas" that are depicted or taught in them, but stories with little or no historical reality in them? Some are inclined to speak of Genesis 1–11 as "primeval history" (with little historical value) while Genesis 12–50 is "patriarchal history" (more historical basis). We will come back to this point later.

The student of Genesis 1–11 should not be surprised to find that paleontology and archaeology have not recovered material facts to support all the data mentioned in early Genesis. The Scripture has a message to tell, and it tells its redemptive message in narratives that read like "factual" history. Perhaps an illustration may help at this point. When one drives through a large national park, the driver does not see all the plants and animals that exist in the park. The road is such a narrow band. Conversely, those who study the park extensively will not encounter very frequently that which stays close to the road, that narrow band.

Genesis 1–11 tells stories that have a specific focus (the "narrow road"). Various sciences may very well investigate the wide ranges of the creation and its various aspects as God's world existed many, many years ago (the "large park"). If historical research has not discovered Cain, for example, that is understandable. Conversely, one must not extrapolate what "early man" was like, for example, from the brief phrase "Cain was a tiller of the ground" (Gen. 4:2), as if all early mankind was settled agriculturalists.

This is not to say that Scripture and science belong in two watertight compartments. Divine redemption and revelation occur in this creation, in a history and in a cosmos that is common to both the Christian and the non-Christian alike. The study of this world in all its marvelous dimensions requires for the confessing Christian the usage of the Scripture as the proper lenses or eyeglasses in order to see more clearly what God reveals in the world. Such study can be very useful even in the reading of Scripture because the inspired text has a context in time and space, in history and in culture.

The Christian is therefore not afraid to ask questions or even to listen to what the various sciences are saying, provided he always remembers that science must remain modest in all of its claims of what "really happened" in the earliest eras of creation's history. The Christian must always remember that there are no neutral facts anywhere in the creation. Even Biblical "facts" are not neutral! "The heavens are telling of the glory of God; and their expanse is declaring the work of His hands," says Psalm 19:1. Romans 1:19–20 adds the following:

"Because that which is known about God is evident within them; for God made it evident to them. For since the creation of the world His invisible attributes, His eternal power and divine nature, have been clearly seen, being understood through what has been made, so that they are without excuse."

Creation is truly a "most elegant book" that speaks clearly of God the Creator. Scripture is also a most elegant book, but one which speaks "more clearly and fully" to its readers about all that is "necessary for us to know in this life," to the glory of God and our salvation (Belgic Confession, Article 2).

Genesis 1–11: revisiting the chapters

If we allow the Scripture to set its own agenda and take note of its own divisions, then it is questionable to see Genesis 1–11 as the best unit for study. Why make the major break at the end of chapter 11 when Abram is introduced already within Genesis 11? Does he not belong with what follows in chapter 12?

The fullest account of the creation week is given to us in Genesis 1:1 through 2:3. The chapter break is not always that helpful to the reader. When seen as a whole unit, Genesis 1:1–2:3 describes in a very structured, orderly way God's putting into place everything that pertains to our world and our time. The stage is constructed and its players are placed on that creational stage through the power of God's creative word.

Then in Genesis 2:4 we read, "This is the account . . ." The word *account* is translated as *generations, history,* even *record* in other translations. It is an important word that occurs at key places throughout the rest of Genesis. The reader of Genesis can find 10 *account* or *generation* sections:

1. 2:4–4:26: the account of paradise, the fall into sin, enmity between brothers, and the line of Cain.
2. 5:1–6:8: Adam's line through Seth; God's "grief" concerning the human race.
3. 6:9–9:29: Noah, and the woman's seed saved in the flood.
4. 10:1–11:9: Noah's sons; God fills the cleansed world.
5. 11:10–26: Shem, and the blessing of Noah at work.
6. 11:27–25:11: Terah; the blessing of Shem is fulfilled in the son Isaac.
7. 25:12–18: Ishmael (Abraham's other son).
8. 25:19–35:29: Isaac's blessing is fulfilled.
9. 36:1–43: Esau (Isaac's other son).
10. 37:1–50:26: Jacob; Israel is saved by God through Joseph in Egypt.

This appears to be the way that Genesis organizes itself. With each account ("generations") there is a narrowing process, each one giving us more details and characterizations as God moves His covenant of grace along toward the coming of the Lord Jesus Christ. Therefore, Genesis does not think along the lines of "primeval history" and then "patriarchal history." This might be the way some scholars have construed the book of Genesis, but this does not appear to be the way Genesis is itself arranged.

At times the central figure in the particular *generation* is not the one named at the beginning of the *generation*. For example, Abraham is the central figure in the *generation* of Terah, and Joseph plays a very prominent role in the *generation* of Jacob. We thus begin to see immediately that Genesis does not give us first of all biographies of Bible heroes, or merely stories of interesting people who lived a long time ago in the ancient Near East. Rather, the stories of Genesis move us along redemptive history, from a beginning toward an end point.

Genesis 1–11: God's work in history

We have noted how God's inspired Word tells us only what it wants us to know about how the sovereign God has worked in history. All of the rest of the Bible understands that the characters and the events recorded in Genesis 1–11 are real people and actual events. We can return to this point in later lessons where such is appropriate. If any one should make the claim that the "assured results of science" have made it impossible for us to believe, for example, that Adam and Eve were our first parents, specially created by the hands of God, then the confession that Scripture is its own interpreter is denied. Romans 5 and I Timothy 2 appeal precisely to the reality of Adam as covenant head and representative for the whole human race. The Bible, in its totality and its unity, lays down its own directions for reading.

Genesis 1–11 speaks of people, places and events that are real. It tells us its history in stories. We should not be afraid to call the early chapters of Genesis "stories," provided that we understand them to relate to the reader facts that the rest of Scripture teaches to be facts. Always check out how a scholar or any writer is using his terms: how does he define the important words he uses?

At the same time, let us remember that the facts of redemptive history are not told to us to make us more intelligent, but they are recorded to make us believers in the God who has entered into this creation in order to save it from sin and death.

Points to ponder and discuss

1. How important are our presuppositions about the Bible in our reading of the Bible? What must we believe about the Bible when we read and study it? See Belgic Confession, Articles 2, 3, 5, 7; Westminster Confession, Chapter 1.
2. Check out, if you are able, some Bible encyclopedias or Bible introductions to see what some of the critical understandings are of the origins of the Pentateuch, including Genesis. Why do many scholars today reject the idea that Moses is the human author of the Pentateuch? Did Jesus accommodate Himself to the beliefs of His day in speaking of Moses as the writer of the Pentateuch, when in fact Moses was not the writer? If so, what does this do to our view of Jesus Christ?
3. The Bible as a text, a body of literature, shows many of the features that belong to texts. Some have advocated that we should read the Bible "just like any other book." Evaluate this statement. What is true and what is not true about this statement?
4. What are some of the challenges that the sciences today raise in our reading of Genesis? How can the study of history, archaeology, and other sciences actually help us in reading the Bible? What other parts of the Bible have "questions" raised about them because of what some scientists are saying?
5. Read John 20:30–31 and 21:25. How can these verses help us ask the right kinds of questions about the rest of Biblical history, including Genesis 1–11?
6. Some say that only the teachings ("ideas") of the Bible are important but not its historicity. Evaluate such a suggestion. How important is the factor of history and historicity in the Bible? See John 1:14; I John 1:1ff.

Lesson 2

The First Day

Read Genesis 1:1–5

In the beginning God created His kingdom. Genesis 1:1 reveals to us that the totality of all that exists was created by only one almighty Being, namely, God Himself. Very clearly God makes Himself the first subject of Genesis and thus of the Bible itself. Before anything created was or came into existence, God is and exists sufficient unto Himself and for Himself. Read Isaiah 40 and several following chapters. These Biblical passages make it clear that God is the First and the Last in creation.

All things He created

Genesis 1:1 tells us that God created "the heavens and the earth." Later on in this chapter we learn that the sky (firmament) is called "the heavens" (or "heaven"), and the dry land is called "the earth." But we would be misreading Scripture if we understood Genesis 1:1 to be saying nothing more than that in the beginning God created "the sky and the dry land." Rather, the two things mentioned in verse 1 ("the heavens and the earth") refer to the totality that belongs to a particular category, in this case, that which was created. If, for example, the Bible mentions "day and night," it refers to the totality of a unit of time. Or again, when we read in Zephaniah 1:12 that the LORD will "do nothing, either good or bad," the words "good" and "bad" when read together speak of a totality. In Isaiah 44:24 we read, "I am the LORD, who has made all things, who alone stretched out the heavens, who spread out the earth by Myself." Notice in this Isaiah verse the words "alone" and "by Myself."

The Christian Church confesses, however, that this God (the word in the original is the more general name for Deity, i.e., *'Elohîm*) is one Being, three Persons. In verse 2 the Spirit of God is seen hovering over the great deep, demonstrating already the non-created nature of the Spirit as well as His splendid sovereignty over the creational elements. The Spirit of God and the Word (the Son) of God are also active Persons in creating all things when Psalm 33:6 says, "By the word of the LORD were the heavens made, their starry host by the breath of His mouth." The word for "breath" can also mean "Spirit" or "wind."

Furthermore, God the Son is also active in creation of the kingdom over which God rules. John 1:10 tells us that the world was made through Him. Paul reminds the Colossian church (and us as well!) that "by Him all things were created: things in heaven and on earth, visible and invisible. . . all things were created by Him and for Him. . . . and in Him all things hold together" (Col. 1:16, 17). This teaching is again underscored by Hebrews 1:2, which says regarding Jesus Christ the Son, God "appointed heir of all things, and through whom He made the universe." These are powerful statements! Jesus Christ, God the Son, created everything, keeps it all together, gives all things meaning and purpose, and seeks to direct all things for Himself, for the glory of God the Father.

"In the beginning"

If time is integral to the creation order itself, it is somewhat problematic to speak of a "before" the creation. What was there before the "in the beginning" of creation, except God Himself? Yet He is above, before, underneath, and after time, space, and all things. We use language to describe God's Being and His activity, sometimes in ways that cannot fully grasp all that God is. Before there was anything, there was, and is, and always will be the great Creator, God.

If we believe that the creation account here (and we are not forgetting the further revelation of Genesis 2) is being put by Moses before God's people in the time of the wilderness wanderings, then the revelation of Genesis 1:1 is extremely significant. In Moses' day (as today!) people believed in many gods. In effect, this leads to a "multi-verse" of conflicting deities and different law-givers (and thus different laws). Genesis 1:1 reveals that there is only one God, only one Law-giver, and thus His Law-word is one, coherent, unified, sensible, and ultimately good. One God, one kingdom!

Creation, then a gap?

Some students of the Bible suggest that the creation account of Genesis one represents the restoration of a world that became chaotic "between" verses one and two. First, God created all things, but then the world fell into a disorganized state of affairs. This theory makes room, of course, for the world to be very, very old, and thus compatible with the claims of many scientists who insist on a universe that is at least six billion years old. The very ancient remains of "human ancestors" represent evidence from that earlier, fallen world, it is said. What God is doing in Genesis 1:3ff. is actually reordering or reconstructing a universe that had become disordered. Thus, it is claimed, there is a "gap" between verses one and two, a gap that represents a great amount of time. After all, not everything that has happened in the history of the world has been recorded in the Bible for us (which, of course, is true, but not necessarily applicable at this point in the text!).

However, there is nothing in the text that warrants such a view. The text in the original language does not use a verbal form that would indicate "became" (thus "the earth *became* formless and empty"). When Adam was created, are we to understand that he lived in a creation already billions of years old, with the remains of pre-Adamite beings and many skeletal remains of thousands of creatures already in the ground? Was the first world that was destroyed (in the "gap") not so good, while the world created in Genesis was "very good?" The Scriptural text does not allow us to say that "God created all things in six days, except for…" Rather, close attention to the text leads the reader to another kind of conclusion.

Unformed and unfilled

In the original language, the last word of verse 1 is "the earth," and the first word of verse 2 is "the earth." This points out that the Bible is turning its attention to the concerns of what God did in the creation of the earth. The realm called "the heavens" is thus set aside for the moment. This is the place of God's throne room, the place where the seraphim, the cherubim, the archangels, and thousands of angels wait upon the Lord in the great heavenly council, praising and glorifying Him forever. In Psalm 89:11 tells us that both the heavens and the earth belong to God because He has founded it. The heavens and the earth—these are the kingdom over which He is absolute Sovereign.

But there is more to consider. Psalm 115:16 reminds us that the highest heavens belong to the LORD, but the earth He has given to man. Thus the text turns our attention immediately to "the earth." Within God's kingdom we are given a home, a place, space in which we are called to glorify God and enjoy Him forever. This is the area of man's activity, the place where the image-bearer of God will carry out his service for, and worship of, the living God.

This earth is described in verse 2 as being initially "formless and empty" (or void). This has led some to describe the initial creation as being a "chaos." Such a term is most unfortunate because it suggests that matters were out of control, as if no one was in charge of things. Perhaps the word "chaos" reminds us of the children's playroom after an afternoon when the three-year old and the five-year old have been in it!

God did not create a chaotic mess. In fact, the rest of the creation week will be God's work that will *divide* the various areas of the earth (understood broadly as that all that which is not "the heavens," God's special throne room), and then He will *populate* the areas that have been formed through division. What is formless receives form through separation on roughly the first three days, and what is empty receives occupants on the last three (or four) days of the creation week. The wisdom of divine design is about to be held up before the believers' eyes! Thus "formless and empty" are not seen as something inherently evil, but the phrase describes "the earth" as it was in the beginning, at that initial point when our God brought it into existence.

Day one – one day

It is inevitable that the question arises here as to the nature of the days of the creation week. Does the word *day* represent a long period of time (an age of, say, millions or billions of years)? Does it mean a period of 24-hours, nothing more and nothing less, as we experience that today? Or, is the creation week of six days of work and the seventh day of rest merely a literary, quasi-poetic, account of the beginning, and therefore not at all descriptive of how the world began?

An exhaustive discussion of every question involved in this topic goes beyond the primary concerns of this Bible study. However, this writer takes the position that the days of Genesis 1 are to be understood not as long periods of time ("ages") since the original language has devises for expressing long periods of time, and those vocabulary devises are not used in Genesis 1. This writer understands that the days of Genesis 1 are ordinary days of alternating evenings and mornings, real periods of time that succeeded each other in the very beginning of God's kingdom. Even many scholars who do not believe that the days of Genesis are real and ordinary days will admit that the text, on any surface reading, conveys that idea to the reader. In other words, the "plain sense reading" clearly pushes the reader to this conclusion: the days of Genesis 1 are real days of time and space.

But there are more reasons that may be adduced in support of this reading. Read Exodus 20:11 and 31:17, for example. Scripture reminds us that God created the world and all that is in it in the space-time period of six days, with the seventh day being set aside as the day of rest (we'll examine that more closely in a later lesson). Of course, the primary analogy being set forth here is the six plus one pattern that defines the human week, not primarily the length of the Genesis 1 days. However, if the days of Genesis 1 have no analogy to the days of the week as we experience the week, then God is drawing an analogy to something that, in effect, never happened. This would be a strange reading of the fourth commandment indeed!

Secondly, the argument that is occasionally heard that to God a day is a thousand years, is not an accurate reading of the text. Read II Peter 3:8 (cf. Ps. 90:4). It says that "with the Lord one day is as a thousand years, and a thousand years as one day." Notice the comparative word as. It reveals to us again (as we need to be reminded of this fact) that our sovereign King is above all limitations and restrictions that time may impose upon us as creatures. God created time, He controls all time, He is involved with us in time, but He is not restricted by time. God does not wear a wristwatch, nor is He constrained by human calendars! "His purposes will ripen fast, unfolding every hour." He can do whatever He wills in a split second, or He can work out His plan over many millennia. But it was His good pleasure to create all things in the space of six days, real and actual space-time days of successive evenings and mornings.

Thirdly, it must be admitted that the word "day" (*yôm* in the original language) can have other meanings, even within Genesis 1. Elsewhere in the Old Testament the "day of the LORD" phrase, so common in the prophets, takes us beyond a strictly 24-hour period. Genesis 1:5 (cf. vs. 14, 16, 18) even draws our attention to two uses of the word. The light by itself is called "day," while the evening and the morning constitute the period we know as a "day." (Even the English language uses the same distinction.) So, the reader must be sensitive to context and usage of a word within that context. Our concern at this point is the usage of the word *day* that concludes the description of each successive period of creational activity.

Fourthly, each of the six creation days has a numerical adjective before it ("second," "third," etc.). By analogy with other portions of Scripture (for example, Num. 7:12–78; cf. Zech. 14:7), when such a construction is used, the days are understood to be ordinary days. When the plural "days" is used elsewhere in the Old Testament, the understanding is that they are normal, ordinary periods of time we recognize as days.

Fifthly, the text of Genesis 1 defines these days as "evening... and... morning." This restricts the understanding of what a day is. Obviously, Genesis was not written at the North or South poles, where an evening or morning can be quite long at certain times of the year! Genesis was written by Moses, whose feet stood on the ground of the ancient Near East. A day is composed of an evening period (darkness), followed by the period of morning (daylight). In Daniel 8:26 there is the reference to evenings and mornings (in connection with sacrifices); these are clearly understood are normal days.

Finally, the references to "seasons," "days," and "years" in Genesis 1:14 point to units of time measurement which were understood and were well-known by the reader. As mentioned above, the plural form here for "day" points to the meaning of "day" as that of a normal, ordinary day.

The points noted above, when put together, have an accumulative effect. They point us in the direction of understanding the creation week as being six real and actual days, in immediate succession to each other, days in which God separated the parts of the earth into their respective portions and then populated those separate portions with the creatures that make up His royal realm.

There are those who see Genesis 1:1ff. merely as a literary panel. They come to this conclusion from at least one of two directions (not always mutually exclusive, but certainly distinguishable). Some say that "the assured results" of science tell us that the world, the stars, and all living creatures could not have come into being at the instant God gave His word. Others would argue that the account of creation as given in Genesis 2:4ff. is historical, while Genesis 1 has only a theological, perhaps polemical, point to make. In other words, there may be exegetical (textual) reasons for seeing Genesis 1 as not literal, although it is still very important for what it reveals about God's creation and sovereignty. In several later lessons, we will give more attention to these suggestions.

"And God said"

The first subject of the Bible is God, and the first Speaker of the Bible is God as well. By His words, "Let there be light," He wills light into existence. So it will be with the other events of the creation week and with the other elements that are made in these first six days.

Read verses 3, 6, 9, 11, 14, 20, 22, 24, 26, 28, and 29. Here we read the recurring phrase "And God said," or

"God blessed them and said." Creation begins with divine, royal words. Later, at Mount Sinai, the Ten Words will come from the heavenly King, covenantally binding Israel as a people, divinely-created, to their royal Master and sovereign Father. In the beginning God's word creates His kingdom; at Sinai God's word creates His kingdom of priests, Israel.

The first word: light

God is light, and in Him there is no darkness at all (cf. Ps. 27:1; 36:9; John 1:3; 12:35). This light of Genesis 1:3, however, is a created phenomenon, the first of God's gifts to the creation. By creating light first before the light-givers or the light-bearers of the fourth day, God is showing us that the sun (or suns) is not the ultimate source of light. The ancients worshiped the sun as a god because they saw it as a source of their life and wellbeing. In connection with the creation of light first, E. J. Young (*In the Beginning*, p. 40) says the following, "Light is the foundation of all that follows… But that we may understand that light, the necessary foundation for all life, is the gift of God and not of the sun, light is mentioned before the sun." We will more to say about this in connection with the fourth day. In any case, we note that light is created to separate itself from the darkness. God has begun the grand task of removing the formlessness of the earth He created in the beginning.

Points to ponder and discuss

1. II Timothy 3:16–17 tells us that the Scripture is profitable and useful for teaching us the truth so that we may be equipped for every good work. What teachings (doctrines) are positively taught, explicitly or implicitly, in Genesis 1:1? What falsehoods (errors, heresies) are denied or are able to be refuted by Genesis 1:1?

(Think in this connection of atheism, polytheism, deism, pantheism, etc.)

2. Read Colossians 1:15–17 and Hebrews 11:3. Historically the Christian Church has confessed the doctrine of creation *ex nihilo* (out of nothing). How important is this teaching? What challenges in recent times have been raised against this teaching? At what points did God use means and/or material in His creative work?
3. God as the absolute Sovereign of the universe controls all that happens within His kingdom, yet we speak of *miracles* and *providence*. How can we explain what is a divine miracle and what is divine providence?
4. In the Westminster Confession of Faith, Chapter IV ("Of Creation") we read: "It pleased God the Father, Son, and Holy Ghost, for the manifestation of the glory of His eternal power, wisdom, and goodness, in the beginning, to create, or make of nothing, the world, and all things therein, whether visible or invisible, in the space of six days, and all very good." In your own words, what is the Confession here teaching? What does the Confession mean "in the space of six days"? Do Christian churches today need to make even more explicit statements about what they believe about creation, or may there be some freedom of understanding within the wording of the Reformed confessions? Why, or why not?
5. Read John 1:1–5. In what ways is this New Testament passage parallel to the opening verses of Genesis 1? What is the significance to such an introduction to the Gospel of John?
6. What comfort is there in Genesis 1:1 for the believer in the revelation that all things come from God, the only God, the sovereign God?

Lesson 3

Constructing the Creation-Kingdom

Read Genesis 1:6–25

In this lesson we will examine God's handiwork on days two through six. But we will reserve our study of the creation of man (the sixth day) until the following lesson.

The great Creator God created His vast realm in the course of six days, and He reveals that truth to His covenant people through Moses. In telling us the truth God was careful to say it in such a way that we might understand what is critical for Israel and us to be His people, and that we might be even better equipped to serve as the citizens of His kingdom.

Poetry, science, or narrative?

A question that arises in the study of Genesis 1 regards the kind of literature it is. What type of writing is it? Some say that it is poetry. Others argue for prose narrative (i.e., straightforward story). No one would say that Genesis 1 is a science text, but they might look very carefully for ways in which Genesis 1 fits some modern scientific models or categories. Furthermore, some people ask whether we should take Genesis 1 in a *literal* manner or in a *literary* manner, perhaps posing these as necessarily in opposition to each other. Read Genesis 1 again and listen to its content and its cadences. Look for the repeated phrases in the description of God's creative activity.

After reading Genesis 1 again in its entirety, you will notice several repeated elements as the construction of

God's creation-kingdom is described. Not every day has every one of these elements, but many of the days do contain them.

1. God's *speech*: "And God said."
2. The *results* of that speech: "God made... and it was so."
3. God *names* what He has made.
4. An *evaluation* of what happened: "God saw that it was good."
5. The "evening and morning" formula, marking the transitions from day to day.

In this way the inspired writer keeps pressing upon the reader certain critical matters. Genesis 1 is not written in classic poetic style, but neither is it a flat, two-dimensional reporting of "just the facts." God speaks, it happens, He gives it an identity, He judges it good, and then He does it again! He is busy putting together His kingdom in place, stage by careful stage.

So should we approach Genesis 1 *literally*, or should the reader simply note the *literary* formulas and little more? Myth, theology, or science: what's our category?

We should exercise great caution when we attempt to place relatively modern categories of literature upon the written revelation of God. To be sure, we are able to note the distinctive features of Biblical literature in its various types, but the Biblical types of literature do not always fall into hard and fast, ironclad categories. For example, the history of God's covenant people is told in Psalm 78, part of the praise (i.e., poetic) collection of God's Word. But Psalm 78:1–4 gives us certain descriptive words about what Psalm 78 is. It is "instruction," a "parable," "dark sayings of old," etc. We would not deny or even discredit the historical record being sung and retold in Psalm 78, but the reader would be not be surprised to read the account and notice poetic features (e.g., parallelism, emotive language, more colorful description, etc.). Every piece of literature, including the Biblical text, has its own nature, its own genre. But we must clearly remember that the genre (type) of a text does not in itself determine the factual reality of the material in it. Even poetry can tell the reader "what really happened," albeit in the manner of poetry. (Both words *literal* and *literary* come from the same Latin word for "letter," *littera*: what does the text, the *letters*, say?)

As we noted above, Genesis 1 presses upon us certain things about God and His sovereign, wise manner of constructing the vast realm of His creation. Its measured cadences put this chapter somewhere between a straightforward story narrative and poetry. It is certainly a far cry from the elaborate, polytheistic myths of the Babylonians and the Egyptians. Nor is it simply a theological essay, only a statement of ideas that informs the doctrines of the church, but does not describe what the Creator God did in the beginning. Derek Kidner (*Genesis*, pp. 54–55) says that the "march of the days is too majestic a progress to carry no implication of ordered sequence; it also seems over-subtle to adopt a view of the passage which discounts one of the primary impressions it makes on the ordinary reader. It is a story, not only a statement." In other words, "facts" are presented to the reader in a stylized narrative form: in six days God alone created all that exists, all of it was properly ordered, and all of it was very good.

Science cannot ignore what Genesis 1 says. At the same time, Scripture does not answer all the many questions that we could raise. God's Word "sets its own agenda" for us; we do not put an agenda upon the Word. Science must remain modest in its claims of what "really happened" in the earliest eras of time because science does not have all the data necessary to draw its own definitive pictures. Because none of us were there, humble students of God's

Word must listen to the Author of the Word, God Himself, who was actually there "in the beginning." What He says, we believe, even as many questions may come to mind.

Day two (1:6–8): the atmosphere

After the creation of the light, God now proceeds on the second day to create the firmament. The word used here is related to a verb that means to stamp out or to stretch. For example, metals can be pressed out or hammered out to form an overlay or covering (gold, Exod. 39:3; silver, Jer. 10:9; bronze, Num. 16:39). If you were to stand outside on a cloudless day, the sky above would look something like an enormous blue bowl, now inverted over the earth. From the vantage point of one who stands on the ground, this expanse is the place where the sun travels in daily regularity and the moon moves in its regular cycles. This "upside-down bowl" looks as if it had been stamped out or stretched out over us.

The firmament is that expanse that covers the earth. It is the atmosphere that, one might say, lifts the sky above the earth and serves as a kind of boundary between the earth and the "beyond." This is not the precise language of science, because Moses is not speaking here as a scientist. He speaks as a prophet, revealing how God is now putting in the necessary spacing in the earth, spacing required for His kingdom elements on the subsequent days. E. J. Young reminds us that the expanse ("firmament") is "not a material substance, but simply a separation of the waters that adhere to the earth from what is beyond. More than that we cannot say" (*In the Beginning*, p. 44).

Day three (1:9–13): land, seas, and vegetation

The third day of kingdom construction has two points of activity or focus. Verses 9 and 11 both record the important words, "God said." If on the second day God separated the waters, on the third day He now gathers them together into distinct bodies. This now allows the dry land to appear, without which, of course, no land-based life could exist. The seas may later in Biblical revelation come to symbolize the restlessness of the nations, but in the perfect beginning the seas have boundaries, set in place by God.

The various kinds of vegetation (plants, trees, etc.) are said to be produced by the land, and the plants and trees are made "according to their kinds." Admittedly, the ancient world did not work with the precise categories of species that scientists use today, but the ancient peoples knew, for example, the differences between the palm and the oak, the myrtle and the thorn bush. We should also recognize that diversity and differentiation within God's creation is already in place from the very start. It is not the case that all life forms (plant, bird, animal) evolved out of one single primitive cell. Many of God's creatures may be like each other in so many different ways (e.g., they breathe oxygen, have two legs, etc.). But such similarities do not constitute proof of development from the one to the other. Diversity in the plant and animal realms (1:24, 25) of God's creation was from the beginning. "And God saw that it was good" (1:12).

Day four (1:14–19): the light-bearers

Genesis 1:14–19 records the creation of the sun, moon, and stars. But did you notice that the words *sun* and *moon* are not used in this account? There seems to be a reason for such. In the ancient world, the civilization of Moses' day, if you said "sun," the reference would be to the sun god. If one mentioned the "moon," he would be speaking of the moon god. Polytheism (the belief in more than one god) was rampant, and words which to us would not have any association with gods and goddesses, did have such a meaning to the ancients. Perhaps in a very subtle way, God through Moses is pressing an understanding upon us that moves us away from a polytheistic worldview. If the pagans believed in all kinds of myths about their gods and goddesses, then God is giving us a creation account that is very "demythologised." The sun, moon, and stars are not minor deities; they are created by God Himself, and therefore they are His creatures, subject to His control, to His Word, and to His law.

God assigns to the heavenly light-bearers the task of separating day from night and also of governing the day and the night. The sun, moon, and stars are signs for marking "seasons and days and years" (1:14). They are celestial clocks or calendars, one might say, to guide the daily and liturgical lives of God's people. The ancient Hebrews observed a lunar month (new moon festivals), and with the passing of the various months, they would know when particular festivals should be celebrated. Not only do the heavens declare the glory of God (Ps. 19:1), but the sun rules the day and runs like a bridegroom-champion across the sky (Ps. 19:4b–6). The pagan world would turn these heavenly beings into deities and worship them, but God's Word tells us that they were made to regulate our time.

Day five (1:20–23): creatures of the seas and skies

On the second day of the creation week God formed the expanse which separates the "waters below" from the "waters above." Now He proceeds to fill these areas of His kingdom. The water of the seas now swarms with living creatures (fish, sea mammals, etc.) while the skies over the earth receive all the varieties of birds. Again we hear the text underscore the fact that God made all these creatures "according to their kind." Plus, God evaluates all that He made as good.

We should also note that the word *create* is used in verse 21. In this context the verb *create* almost certainly does not mean "out of nothing" as it does in verse 1. Later in verse 25 the text says that "God made" the wild animals, and this strongly implies that God used the material of the earth to form these creatures. In a parallel manner, God creates mankind, but Genesis 2 will make clear that the dust of the ground is the raw material, one might say, for making man. In any case, God fills the seas and the skies with their respective populations.

God also creates the sea monsters, the "great creatures of the sea." This is also a significant statement. The pagan world lived in fear of a great sea monster, a monstrous serpent-like creature of the ocean depth. (There is no need to speculate on what species this might be!) Of course, it is true that the oceans and seas contain some remarkable creatures. The blue whale, for example, is the largest mammal in the world, and it is not land-based. But the inspired text confronts us with the truth that all creatures come from the creative and powerful word of God. Therefore, one should not stand in fear of them. In fact, these creatures are part of the grand chorus of creation that praises the LORD. Psalm 148:7 says, "Praise the LORD from the earth, you great sea creatures and all ocean depths." Then the Psalm adds this in verse 10, "wild animals and all cattle, small creatures and flying birds."

Genesis 1:22 also says that God *blessed* these sea and sky creatures. He even addresses them with a "command" to be fruitful so that they may fill the seas and the earth! We will say more about this in the lesson that deals with the creation of man. It is sufficient to point out here that the statement about God's blessing is that it is the very thing that empowers the creatures to be so fruitful. Without God's blessing nothing can ever prosper. That will be true for humans and all human endeavors; it is also true for the non-human creation. "Thy Spirit, O Lord, makes life to abound" (see Psalm 104).

Eph 1:4 God chose us before the foundations of the world.

Day six (1:24–25): all kinds of land creatures

We will, as was said earlier, reserve our study of the creation of man until later. Day six, like day three, records the expression, "God said," more than once (see 1:24, 26, 29). Thus there seems to be a multiple focus to this day as there was to day three. As day three was concerned with the formation of seas and dry land, so day six is concerned with the filling of the dry land, first with the land creatures as well as with man himself.

We note that the various land creatures include everything from the large beasts down to the creeping things. Animals that will later be suitable as clean animals for sacrifice are now made "living beings." But, in addition, beasts not clean in the Old Testament era are made, including the animals that glide and creep over the earth's surface. Nothing is inherently evil or unclean in the beginning. In fact, the inspired writer Moses reminds us that God's own evaluation of all the animals of the dry land is also "good" (1:25).

The stage is now set for the last (but not least!) element to be created and thus complete the creation-kingdom of God. Up to this point the construction work of creation has proceeded without any conflict and without problems. God's words bring about in perfect order all that His sovereign will has desired. He scans His handiwork, and He exclaims, "I really like what I have done. Excellent work!" Certainly the heavenly choirs must have sung out His praises as the appropriate worshipful response.

Points to ponder and discuss

1. Read II Corinthians 12:1–6. Paul speaks of a man (Paul himself?) who is caught up to "the third heaven" (12:2) or "to paradise" (12:4). Where can we say this place is? Does the rest of the Bible give us any insight into what

the third heaven or paradise is? For this answer, read also Ephesians 4:10; Hebrews 4:14; 7:26.

2. One frequently hears weather announcers referring to "Mother Nature." Do you ever hear on TV or radio weather reports mention of "Father God?" What do people mean by "Mother Nature?" Is this some kind of modern goddess? What should be the attitude or response of Christians to this "Mother Nature" deity?
3. The Belgic Confession in Article 2 says that we know God "by two means: First, by the creation, preservation, and government of the universe; which is before our eyes as a most elegant book, wherein all creatures, great and small, are as so many characters leading us to see clearly the invisible things of God, even His everlasting power and divinity, as the apostle Paul says (Rom. 1:20)." Why does the natural man deny this? What kinds of things should a Christian point out to those who do not believe that the creation points to the existence of the Creator God?
4. In the light of what is revealed in Genesis 1 about the creation week, how important are Christian education and a Christian perspective in education and in all the sciences? What can an unbeliever truly "know" about this world which God created?
5. When the Bible says that the various plants and animals were created "according to their various kinds," how is evolution already being implicitly addressed and refuted?
6. From the orderliness of the creation account, what things do we learn about the nature of our God? See also Psalms 104 and 136; Isaiah 40:21, 22; 45:18 (cf. I Cor. 14:33, 40).

literal

—ESV

English Standard Version

NKJ

majority text rule

Lesson 4

Creation of the Kingdom's Crown

Read Genesis 1:26–31; Psalm 8; Hebrews 2:5–9

We give the creation of man in the image of God separate consideration because of the important role that God assigns to man. He alone is made the image-bearer of God! The last creature made is the first citizen of the kingdom of God on earth!

The plural of majesty?

The name that is used for God throughout Genesis 1 is *'Elohîm*. Spelled in this way, it is plural in form (in some contexts the word could even mean "gods"), and this plural form is often described as the "plural of majesty," a kind of divine, imperial word for God (or Deity). This is probably an adequate explanation in most contexts. But in verse 26 we read, "Then God said, 'Let us make man in our image, in our likeness." We note the use of the words *us* and *our.* It is not enough to say that this is simply because the name of God is plural in form. Is God speaking to Himself or to the heavenly court or council?

Some have argued that God is here addressing the angelic council. From other portions of Scripture we read of such a court. Isaiah 6 tells us of the awesome seraphim, the six-winged creatures around the heavenly throne, creatures that perpetually cry out, "Holy, holy, holy, LORD Almighty! The whole earth is full of His glory!" Ezekiel 1 and elsewhere in the Old Testament describe the cherubim, composite creatures who both guard the heavenly throne and bear up the heavenly throne. In addition, God's heavenly court contains thousands of archangels and angels, heavenly creatures that adore Almighty God and readily do His will. Is God addressing these creatures when He says, "Let us make man in our image"?

Verses 26, 27 reveal to us that mankind is made in God's image, not in the image or likeness of any other creature. God's statement at this point thus takes us beyond the "plural of majesty" understanding to reveal to us a statement within the Godhead. The fuller revelation of all Scripture at this point would be needed to flesh out what this means. Suffice it at this point to say that we have here, already in Genesis 1, a shadow of the Biblical teaching regarding the Trinity. God is one Being, eternally existent as three distinct Persons: Father, Son, and Holy Spirit. Each Person is God, but we do not worship three gods. The Belgic Confession, Article 9, says, "From this saying, Let *us* make man in *our* image, it appears that there are more persons than one in the Godhead; and when He says, *God* created, He signifies the unity. It is true, He does not say how many persons there are, but that which appears to us somewhat obscure in the Old Testament is very plain in the New." Other portions of Scripture cast their light upon other parts of Scripture, because it is one Word of God. Scripture interprets Scripture.

Image and likeness of God

When we reflect upon the nature of the creatures that God has made up to this point, we can observe that there is increasing sophistication and complexity to what God has made. Of course, any cell or molecule is incredibly intricate and complex, as any scientist can well admit. But, notice that on the third day, vegetation of all kinds is created, and these plants and trees will produce food for the beasts, the birds, and man himself (1:29–30), those beings created on days five and six. Yet only man is described as being created in the image of God, after His likeness. Whatever image and likeness may mean, man is in this regard a unique creature.

Older exegesis of this passage attempted (without success) to draw a distinction between *image* and *likeness*. But this is not warranted. The Hebrew language uses parallelism with great frequency, and the point is not to draw attention to how the two parts of the parallelism are different, but to say something twice (even three times on some occasions!) that reinforces one thought. To be sure, the one part of the parallelism might enhance or amplify the other parallel statement, but the reader is not to dwell on how much distinction can be made. Image and likeness thus together speak of man as fully representative of God the King, his Maker.

An image is a reflection or copy of the original. When God looked upon the man, He saw His own glory and perfections reflected. In the ancient world of Moses' day, when a king would conquer a certain land or territory, the conquering king would often have statues of himself set up in the conquered land, to be an abiding statement of who the owner was and who was in charge. For example, in the former Soviet Union statues and pictures of Lenin could be found in all the major cities of the Union, mute evidence of whose philosophy attempted to rule the people's lives. Thus, in making man in His image, according to His likeness, God is saying, "This world is My world. The universe and all that is in it is My kingdom. Let no one challenge that!" What a high position God created us to have in the beginning! This position of man as image-bearer already anticipates the second of the Ten Commandments, "You shall not make for yourself any graven image for worship." Man is already created to be God's image! We are called to bear God's image, not make images of Him.

"Made lower than angels"

Psalm 8 is one of the few Psalms in the Bible that have no notes of sadness or lament within it. It begins and ends with a ringing doxology of praise to the LORD on account of His majestic name. The inspired psalmist has picked up the revelation of Genesis 1, focussed on certain key elements in it, and set the message to music (N.B. "for the director of music"). The majesty of the heavenly King is seen in that He has made a vast universe. The heavens clearly testify to this truth (cf. Ps. 19:1). Yet in the midst of all this is man (8:4–5), a small being when compared to the immensity of the heavenly bodies. Remarkably, the smallest members of the human race ("children and infants") have the capacity to utter praise to God. Even they can silence God's enemies! See how our Lord Jesus Christ recalled this psalm when He is confronted by His enemies after He healed the blind and the lame in the Temple (Matt. 21:16).

But this psalm also points out that man is made "a little lower than the heavenly beings" (the Greek Old Testament translates the Hebrew word here, *'Elohîm*, as "angels"). God the Creator and man the creature are truly distinct. They are not two separate entities on one grand "chain of Being." Yet the position given to man is critical. Earlier we mentioned the mighty seraphim and cherubim, the obedient archangels and angels. These constitute the powerful "hosts of heaven." But underneath them God has created mankind, male and female, and we are also called to serve as the earthly contingent, a regiment of the Lord's army, that obeys God willingly and readily here. That man is made a "little lower than the angels" is thus not a "put-down," but it is to know where God has placed us in the ranks that serve Him. "Thy will be done, on earth as willingly as the angels obey in heaven," we pray.

"Yet crowned with glory and honor"

God made mankind to rule the kingdom. Of course, this

cannot be understood in an ultimate or absolute sense. God will always remain the Supreme Monarch over His creation. But something of a hierarchy is established here: man is over the fish, the birds, and every beast of the land. Nothing that was made was excluded from man's responsibility in terms of man's calling to govern (Ps. 8:6–8). Creatures are subordinate to mankind, while mankind is subordinate to God Himself. This is God's glorious gift to us in the beginning: He honors us by making us kings and queens on the earth. What a remarkable calling!

This is tied in with the image of God, it seems to me, and so we return to that topic for the moment. Admittedly, much has been written on what the image of God in man means. Space does not allow us to enter into the intricacies of that immense discussion. Two New Testament passages do, however, throw some light on what is associated with the image of God. In Ephesians 4:24 Paul speaks of the new self, "created to be like God in true righteousness and holiness." God's grace renews what was lost, sinful, and dead. In addressing the Colossians about the new self (Col. 3:10), Paul says that this new self is "being renewed in knowledge in the image of its Creator." The reader should also reflect on what is said in the Heidelberg Catechism, Lord's Day 3; Belgic Confession, Article 14; Canons of Dort, III–VI, Article 1; and Westminster Confession of Faith, Chapter IV.2.

Whatever else may be said about the image of God in man, mankind was crowned with true righteousness, that is, a perfect relationship with God, one in full conformity with the will and plan of God. Man in the beginning knew what was right, and he could execute what was just. Man was a *king*.

God also crowned man with holiness. This means that man was separated away from anything that might be sinful (he was made knowing no sin!), so that he could serve in the very presence of God. Man was a *priest*, and the entire creation was like a glorious temple (cf. Ps. 29:9; Hab. 2:20). Though God be enthroned in heaven, man stood before Him in creation as the high priest would later stand before the Ark of the Covenant in the tabernacle and then the Temple.

Finally, God honored man in the beginning with knowledge. Man knew God, and he had the law of God written in his heart (see Rom. 2:14, 15). In the beginning man possessed the insights to fulfill his calling within the creation-kingdom. Man knew how to rule as king, and he knew how to minister before God's face as a priest. Of course, man's knowledge of reality and God's knowledge of reality are not of the same type. God always knows all things in every perfect way, while man is necessarily limited. But in the beginning man was crowned with the divine gift of understanding and wisdom. Man was a *prophet*.

Thus the original calling of man (king, priest, prophet) anticipates the kind of Savior we would need, the office He would have to fulfill, and the tasks He would be required to accomplish in saving lost humanity and redeeming a fallen world. The first man becomes the "blueprint" for the last Man, Jesus Christ.

Male and female He created them

Genesis 1 does not go into the particulars of the creation of mankind, the man and the woman. Nor does it elaborate on the relationship between the man and the woman. All this comes in Genesis 2, and so we postpone for the moment our discussion of this subject.

Genesis 1:26, 27 focuses on the relationship of humanity to God. The reader should note the fact that in 1:27 the text gets somewhat lyrical and poetic. The verse has three lines, in which the important operative word *create* is used in each line. Mankind is composed of male and female members, and both are created in the image of God. In the beginning male and female enjoyed the dignity of true righteousness, holiness, and knowledge as they lived in the kingdom of God, seeking to fulfill their calling before His face. In the creation of mankind, God has reached the crowning moment of the week.

Benediction as the task begins

On the fifth day the fish and birds had received God's blessing in order that they might increase and fill the waters and the skies. Now again God pronounces a benediction, so that, what reads like a command, is in fact a blessing that will enable the image-bearing male and female to accomplish the office and calling at hand. Blessing suggests the gift of fertile power that produces fruitfulness and prosperity. None of God's rich gifts to us will profit us without His blessing (see Heidelberg Catechism, Lord's Day 50). St. Augustine once prayed, "Give, O Lord, what You ask, and then ask whatever You will." What God commands us in the mandates of our office, He first supplies to us in His loving favor.

The blessing of God follows in very logical order: fruitfulness leads to the increase in numbers, which in turn leads to filling of the earth, which in turn enables mankind to subdue and rule all things.

Genesis 1:28 is sometimes called the "cultural mandate." I prefer to call it the "dominion mandate," because of the call to subdue and rule the whole of the earth. Again, this subject is much discussed, and we will return to it from time to time. But let it be said that mankind is blessed in order that by wise and prudent work and management, he could develop from the resources of this vast creation-kingdom those things that would be beautiful, useful, holy, and wonderful gifts for the Giver, cultural items that could be offered in thanksgiving and gratitude to the God of our creation, the One from whom all blessings flow.

"But we see Jesus"

Read Hebrews 2:5–9 again. The line from Genesis 1, to Psalm 8, and then to Jesus Christ is made clear, and it needs to be made clear because the high position and marvelous calling given to man in the beginning was lost by the rebellion and sin of our first parents. The gospel message receives its shape from the message of Genesis 1. What man was, what man had, and thus all that man lost, is retrieved by another Man, but One who is more than a mere man. Therefore, Genesis 1 is a very real part of the Gospel. The good news of salvation already begins to be sounded in Genesis 1, long before we arrive at the manger in Bethlehem. The only Man truly in charge of the whole world today is Jesus Christ (cf. Matt. 28:16–20). In the gospel, we see Him! He is the One who occupies the threefold office of king, priest, and prophet. The image of God is restored in Him who is the perfect Image of God, our Lord Jesus Christ. You will not understand His Person and His work unless you see how God first crowned us with glory and honor in the beginning.

Points to ponder and discuss

1. What can we say from Scripture about when and why the angels were created? See Hebrews 1; II Peter 2:4; Jude 6 (cf. Belgic Confession, Article 12).
2. How would you explain the doctrine of the Trinity? What Scriptural support would you point to, if you were asked to defend this Christian belief? (See the Westminster Larger Catechism, Q/A 8–11 [with proof-texts])
3. Is there a danger of reading too much doctrine or too little doctrine into individual passages? What role should Christian creeds and confessions have when we study the Bible? What wisdom (or danger) is there in taking

account of what the Christian Church has learned and confessed in the last two thousand years?

4. There have been those who say that the so-called "cultural mandate" has allowed the exploitation of natural resources in the world. In other words, Christians have justified the overuse of the earth's plants, animals, and minerals on the basis of Genesis 1:26–28. Is this true or false? What is the proper attitude, based on Scripture, that we should have toward the resources of God's kingdom? How does Genesis 1:26–28 answer a Hindu (New Agc) worldview? a consumerist mentality? a throwaway society?
5. There are modern philosophies and worldviews around which lower mankind to the level of an animal while animals are elevated to a point of being nearly human (even divine!). What does God's Word in Genesis 1 say to these perspectives? What happens in a society when the created order is turned on its head so that animals are as important as, maybe more important than, human beings?
6. Cultural activities are inescapable. Some Christians say that the Great Commission has now taken over the Cultural (Dominion) Mandate in importance and priority. Do you agree or disagree? Is Genesis 1:28 in any conflict with Matthew 28:18–20? How can Christians sort all of this out in today's world?
7. Some people may wonder occasionally, "Where did we come from? Why are we here?" What is the good news answer of Genesis 1? How important is it today to give attention to the Biblical teaching concerning the *image of God* and our *office* in God's creation-kingdom?

Lesson 5

Made for Man

Read Genesis 1:29–2:3

The crowning moment in the creation week is reached when the sovereign God and King of all makes man in His image. On the sixth day God creates man, blessing him in such a way that he will be able to be fruitful and fill the earth. Thus mankind will be able to serve God by ruling over everything that God had made. Man is created to serve God in terms of his office as king, priest, and prophet—all of this under the sovereign God Himself.

Food for the body . . . and for thought

But the creation of the land animals and man is not all that pertains to the sixth day. God has more to say about the arrangements and the relationships within the kingdom that He has made. Verse 29 tells us that God gives to man food to eat from every plant bearing seed and from every tree that has fruit yielding seed. Then in verse 30 there is added that the beasts and the birds are also given the provision of food from "every green plant."

There are several things to notice here. First of all, this provision of food is described as a gift in the reference to mankind. The verb "to give" is certainly implied in verse 30 (notice the italics in most Bible versions), but it is explicitly stated in verse 29. In addition, both plants and trees are mentioned in regard to man's provisions, but only plants are mentioned with regard to the beasts and the birds. Is this perhaps an anticipation of man's test with regard to a particular tree in Genesis 2–3? Maybe this should not be pressed too hard.

In any case, what is so striking here is the revelation that we have of the King we serve. This account in Genesis 1 stands in stark contrast to the pagan myths current in Moses' day in certain parts of the ancient Near East. Among the Mesopotamian peoples was the myth that man was created when the blood of an evil god spilled on the ground. The Bible says that man was created good, in the image of the Triune God. The pagans believed that the duty of mankind was to provide food for the gods so that they might be satisfied. But here it is the true God who sets out His creation's plants and trees to provide a buffet table, a veritable smorgasbord, for mankind to enjoy. He is concerned that man, being body-and-soul, have the means whereby he might be able to sustain himself. In other words, God feeds us and all creatures with the elements of the world He made. Man is made to rule as a king under God, but even earthly kings need to eat and be refreshed.

Though man's diet is here declared explicitly to be vegetarian, one should not necessarily conclude that man's body is created to be exclusively vegetarian. Later on in Genesis 9:3, following the flood, man is openly given permission to eat meat that has been drained of its blood. We may thus assume that from the beginning man's body was able to accommodate meat, though it was not given to him for food in the beginning.

In addition, the animals and man (created on the same day) are to eat from the same "creational table," and both of them are prevented from shedding blood. Without sin, there is no death in the form of the shedding of blood on the part of the animals nor of man. Though man rules and has dominion over all creatures, this does not allow man to kill the animals of the pre-fallen world. But, then again, there would have been no reason to kill any animal at all (cf. Isa. 11:7; 65:25). Before the fall into sin, the earth was truly a peaceable kingdom.

We noted above that some pagans believed that mankind had the duty of feeding the gods and goddesses. Scripture, on the other hand, teaches us that service to God does not include feeding Him at all. Later in the history of redemption, God prescribes the entire sacrificial system as the ceremonial means of atonement and restoring fellowship between Himself and His people. The altar of sacrifice was a kind of table where the food of God was placed. Yet it was so easy for Israel to assume that she could feed God and in this way earn His favor. But God, the Lord, says in Psalm 50:12–14, "If I were hungry I would not tell you, for the world is mine, and all that is in it. Do I eat the flesh of bulls or drink the blood of goats? Sacrifice thank offerings to God, fulfill your vows to the Most High." We are saved to serve with thanks. We do not serve God in order to be saved.

The function of food

To us food exists in abundant supply. For most of us food markets are close enough to be able to satisfy our every pang of hunger and craving of the palate. This is not true for many millions of people on the earth, and therefore the significance of food and eating may be lost on us in North America. Genesis 1 already portrays man as dependent upon the food that God has made available in the world. Human beings need love, but they cannot "live on love" alone. Nutrients from outside of us must come into us and then be assimilated by our bodies in order to nourish us. Unless you eat, you will soon have no life in you.

Already here in Genesis 1 God is laying down the basic principle that belongs to one of the Christian sacraments, namely, Holy Communion. Jesus Christ made this most pointedly clear in His conversation with the Jews in John 6. Five thousand Jews had been fed by the Lord near the time of the Passover (John 6:4). After He had crossed the Sea of Galilee, the Jews came to Him again, but now He addresses their basic motivations. They were looking for more (miraculous) bread when they should have been seeking Him as Lord and Savior. Jesus tells us, "I am the Bread of life; he who comes to Me shall not hunger, and he who believes in Me shall never thirst" (John 6:35; cf. 6:41, 48, 50, 51). Then our Lord becomes even more graphic when He tells the arguing Jews, "Truly, truly, I say to you, unless you eat the flesh of the Son of Man and drink His blood, you have no life in yourselves. He who eats My flesh and drinks My blood has eternal life, and I will raise him up on the last day" (John 6:53, 54).

Food is God's gift for us in order to live. But the greatest gift of God to His people is His only-begotten Son, in whom we must believe in order to have everlasting life (see John 3:16, 17). He must be taken in by grace through faith, become "part of us," so that the life we live, we live by faith in the Son of God who loved us and gave Himself for us (see Gal. 2:20).

God's final verdict on His work: outstanding!

In earlier verses of Genesis 1 we read about God's evaluation of the particular things He created (see vs. 10, 12, 18, 21, 25). Each particular object is declared to be good in God's eyes. But when the entire kingdom project is completed, it is as if God stands back to admire the totality. He rejoices in all that He has made. The whole is greater than the sum of the parts, so that God can say concerning His handiwork, "That's it! It is very good, absolutely perfect!" The creation is merely a reflection of the nature of the Builder and Creator Himself: a good and perfect God makes everything according to His will, which alone is good and perfect (see Belgic Confession, Articles 1 & 2).

The word for *good* here can also be translated as *beautiful.* Functionally, aesthetically, morally—all the Lord's work is of the finest quality. This is Paradise: a realm under

God that is exquisite in goodness and beauty, entrusted to mankind for its governance, its well-being, and its development.

The seventh day: God's rest

Genesis 2:1 recalls the words of Genesis 1:1. The totality of God's creation-kingdom is now complete. The sixth day brings God's creative activity to an end. His tasks are finished. This is the pattern for mankind as the fourth commandment reminds us when we are told that six days are given to us for labor, six days of every week in which we are to toil and do all our work. How few of us can get everything that needs to be done, actually finished within the six days of the working week! Yet this is the divine pattern that God enjoins upon His covenant people for their own human pattern of activity (Exod. 20:8–11).

By revealing here that God rested or ceased activity, the Scriptures mean that God rested in terms of the activity under discussion, namely that of creating. This does not mean that God ceased doing other things. He continued to uphold everything. His Word continued to sustain and maintain everything in the universe. Without God's Word keeping the heavens and the earth together, then everything would dissolve into chaos, even into nothing. Resting means He stopped creating the new particulars that make up the whole of His kingdom. God enters this rest on the seventh day (Gen. 2:2). This does not mean that God becomes inactive in an absolute sense. Jesus reminds us of the following: "My Father is working until now, and I Myself am working" (John 5:17).

Some have observed that this seventh day does not have the "evening and morning" formula that marks the description of the other six days. It is then said that because the seventh day has no ending but is a long period of time, therefore the other six days are long periods of time. But such is not the case. God enters His own rest on the seventh day: He ceases from making any new elements in His creation. That divine rest is on-going and everlasting. But the normal weekly pattern of days is in place, as Exodus 20:8–11 makes clear for us. The "greater light" (the sun), created on the fourth day, was now in place to rule the daytime. If the seventh day of the first creation week were not a normal earth day, then when did it become so? There is nothing in the text here that requires us to see the seventh day of Genesis 2:2–3 as anything other than like the first six days, days defined as periods of "evening and morning" in orderly sequence.

The Sabbath sanctified

The seventh day is set apart, "made holy" or perhaps "declared holy," because on this last day of the week God rested. The Hebrew word from which we get the word *Sabbath* means "to rest, to cease activity, to stop doing what one has been doing." Exodus 31:12–17 recalls the establishment of the Sabbaths when the LORD through Moses tells Israel that observing the Sabbath is a perpetual sign and covenant. God's people thus are marked before her neighbors as people who copy or model (image) the pattern of the LORD Himself. In "six days the LORD made the heaven and earth, but on the seventh day He ceased from labor, and was refreshed" (Exod. 31:17, NASB). The NIV here says that God "rested," but "refreshed" is more accurate. God never tires (Isa. 40:28), of course, but when He finished His work, He stood back to observe and admire what He made, and He rejoiced. The joy of the LORD is the strength of our life. If God could be "refreshed" by sabbath rest, how much more we can be refreshed if we by faith keep covenant with God in our sabbath rest and worship!

Students of God's Word have noted that the very first full day of man's existence was the Sabbath day. His first full day of life was resting. To put it another way, man's own week *began* with rest (although it was the seventh day of God's week). Today Christians observe the beginning of their week with the sabbath rest. The first day of the week is the Lord's Day (Rev. 1:10) because Jesus arose from the dead on Easter Sunday. He also poured out His Holy Spirit on Pentecost Sunday. The resurrection of Christ and the gift of His Spirit signal the dawn of the new creation. Thus Christians still observe the sabbath rest, but they do so in accordance with the new realities brought about by the new Man, the second Adam, Jesus Christ. We begin the week with Christian rest in order to work in gratitude for the work He has accomplished on our behalf.

Calling the Sabbath a delight

Both Isaiah 56 and 58 speak of observing the Sabbath as holy to God. Isaiah 58:3–7 adds an address concerning the kind of fast that the LORD approves. Food was made for man's life and enjoyment, but Israel thought that by going through the rituals of fasting she could earn God's blessing. But the LORD seeks righteousness and justice, mercy and liberality, especially for those who are oppressed and destitute. God seeks our refreshment and our re-creation as the goal of the Sabbath rest. Thus God's people must keep in mind the holiness of the day *to the LORD*. God's intention is not to make all days profane, outside the concerns of His will, but rather to make the whole week *holy* by doing His will. Isaiah 58:13–14 exhorts us to reject our own will, call the Sabbath holy and a delight, and in this way let the "eternal Sabbath" begin in our hearts already now (see Heidelberg Catechism, Lord's Day 38). He promises then His blessing.

Jesus Christ: Lord of the Sabbath

Part of the blessing mentioned in Isaiah 58:14 is feasting. This lesson has focused on the two of the many things God has made and given to man: food and rest for our refreshment. The Lord Jesus Christ reminds us that the Sabbath (rest) was made for man and not man for the Sabbath. In Matthew 12:1–14 (cf. Mark 2:23–3:6; Luke 6:1–5) there is the account of the disciples plucking grain on the Sabbath in order to eat. This was not the work of harvesting! Food is God's gift to the hungry.

Furthermore, in the Gospel passages mentioned above, our Lord healed on the Sabbath because He was the Lord of the Sabbath. He was not bound by the Pharisees' traditions that had made the Sabbath a day of lifeless restrictions. God intended our refreshment, our re-creation, and our healing in His Sabbath. That's why Christians long for the eternal Sabbath that still awaits the people of God (Heb. 4:1–11). In the new heavens and the new earth the Church will some day feast with the Lamb of God during the joyful Sabbath that will never end. All this He will do. But already in the beginning He has made these for man—and His glory!

Points to ponder and discuss

1. God gave the plants and trees to man for food. In Genesis 9 man is permitted to eat meat. Why are some people vegetarians? Are there legitimate reasons for this practice?
2. Food is God's gift, to be received in thankfulness. Yet in Leviticus 16:29, 31 it says that on the Day of Atonement the people were to deny (or humble) themselves, apparently meaning that they were to fast for that day (cf. Ps. 35:13). It seems that this was the only prescribed fast of the Old Testament. Why do some Christians fast today?
3. Many of the ancient pagan religions treated sexuality as a kind of sacrament. This is why many pagan shrines and

temples had cultic prostitutes. What is a sacrament? What is God's wisdom in using water as the element in holy baptism and food (bread and wine) as the element in Holy Communion?

4. Does God continue to create today? What is the difference between *creation* and *providence*? How do creation and providence relate to each other? Is it important to believe that these are descriptive of two distinct activities of God? See Heidelberg Catechism, Lord's Day 10; Belgic Confession, Article 2; Westminster Confession of Faith, Chapters 4–5.
5. Is the fourth commandment a temporary ceremonial law that passed away with the coming of Jesus Christ, or is it an abiding moral commandment that Christians must observe in gratitude yet today? Is the Lord's Day today the *Christian Sabbath*?
6. Read Heidelberg Catechism, Lord's Day 38. What does God require in the fourth commandment, according to this Catechism? Read Westminster Shorter Catechism, Q/A 57–61 and the Larger Catechism, Q/A 115–121. How are the Heidelberg and Westminster catechisms similar and how are they different (if at all) in both what they require and what they forbid in observance of the fourth commandment?
7. What can Christians positively do today to make the Lord's Day a genuine "Sabbath delight," both for ourselves and our families? How can we witness to our neighbors in the way we keep a Christian Sabbath?

Lesson 6

Placed in the Paradise God Planted

Read Genesis 2:4–17

In the previous lessons we have briefly explored the various parts of the creation that God made on the several days of the creation week. The creation of mankind crowns God's masterful work, and God concludes the week with His rest.

History under the LORD God

In this section of the Bible another name for God begins to be used. In most English Bibles it is "the LORD (Jehovah in the ASV). This is the Name based upon the four letters *YHWH*, the so-called Tetragrammaton (i.e., four-letters). This is the Name that God reveals to Moses in Exodus 3 when he asks God (speaking to Moses from the burning bush) who it is that has sent him. God tells him that "I AM" has sent him. "I AM who I AM" is the God who came to Moses in remembrance of His covenant made with Abraham, Isaac, and Jacob. This is the God who has heard the cries of His people in their slavery in Egypt. This is the God faithful to all of His promises, no matter how many they are or when they were made.

The usage of this personal divine Name at this point in the text is significant. God reveals through Moses that the God who rescued the Israelites from Egyptian cruelty and brought them to Mt. Sinai to give them His covenant law, is the same God who created the world, created mankind, planted the Garden of Eden, and gave man the task of exercising dominion over all creation. The LORD God is thus not a local deity. He is the universal Lord, and He was so from the very beginning! The true God is the only God, and He will not share His glory with any other false gods.

In an earlier lesson we pointed out the presence of the phrase, "This is the account..." (Gen. 2:4; 5:1; 6:9; etc.). The word used for *account* has the sense of "what became of" or "what came forth from." How well that fits here! God describes the creation of the heavens and the earth, and then He proceeds to reveal the history that flowed forth from this creation. As Aalders (*Genesis*, I, 82) says concerning the phrase "when they were created" (Gen. 2:4), the "history of the world commenced the moment creation became an accomplished fact."

One creation, two accounts?

Genesis 2 is often described as a second account of creation, one that disagrees with Genesis 1. But we are not allowed to pit Scripture against Scripture. Instead we are challenged to listen carefully to the text, face the "hard questions," and allow the whole to help interpret and explain the particulars. The clearer parts must shed light on the more difficult to understand passages of God's Word.

In this connection we should remember that Scripture passages at times allow for recapitulation, on the one hand, and anticipation, on the other hand. By recapitulation we mean that the Bible in historical passages sometimes goes back, one might say, and repeats or focuses on things already described and narrated. But the focus will have a distinct purpose, something like casting a spotlight on some person or event that may be almost casually mentioned before. On the other hand, when the Bible anticipates later developments, it may very well give the briefest mention of them at an early point in the story, and only later on expand on them. One might say that certain verses serve as "headlines" (grand summaries) and other verses are "sub-headings" or the fuller story.

Genesis 2:5 is sometimes said to serve as a description of the third day of creation (gathering of waters into seas, appearance of dry land and plants). Along with that view, it is said that ordinary earth processes must have been operative at the time of creation. Admittedly Genesis 2:5–7 raises questions in the mind of the serious student of Scripture. A search of the many commentaries on Genesis shows a wide range of understandings, some of them appear responsible within the contexts of Scripture, while others are quite unacceptable (e.g., Genesis is mythical).

But we may well ask whether ordinary earth processes were operative during the creation of the heavens and the earth. If the creation week were a series of ordinary days in chronological sequence, how could ordinary processes be present, at least for every element of the creation? The creation week is without parallel and without precedence! By extraordinary words, God brought things into being that were not there before.

Genesis 2:5–7 looks both backward and forward to what is in the text of the Bible. Verse 5 refers to the shrub of the field, the wild plants that can grow in a dry region only after they have received sufficient rain. But initially there was no rain! The plant of the field (v. 5) refers to that kind of vegetation that grows best when it is cultivated by human beings. But initially there was no man! Instead of rainfall and mankind there was a stream or great flow of water over the whole surface of the earth. Some translations say *mist* in verse 6, but this is almost certainly not the meaning of the word used in the original language.

If anything, Genesis 2:5–6 sounds more like the condition of the earth on day one or day two rather than day three. Thus this passage is briefly looking back, but it does so in such a way as to anticipate what is to follow. Genesis 1 has man as the final creation of God, but Genesis 2 points to man as the reason for the whole creation. In other words, Genesis 2 picks up the grand story, following a brief recapitulation, and now the text focuses on man. Genesis 1:26–28 tells what man is (image of God) and why man is (to rule and have dominion over God's creation-kingdom). Man is made as the reason for the rest of the creation. He is made as its worker, its tiller, and its caretaker. We will encounter the "plant of the field" again when we come to Genesis 3:18 (God's judgment against Adam).

The formation of man (2:7)

This section is a complement to Genesis 1:27–28, where Scripture reveals that man is created in the image of God, and that man is made male and female. When man was originally created, the Lord God took the dirt on the earth, and He made an "earthling" (the original language has a "play on words" here). God is pictured here as a Potter who molds and shapes the clay of the ground into that creature who will be His image-bearing ruler and governor over the totality of the earth. Someone has suggested that the earth is mankind's "cradle, his home, his grave." It will become his grave after our first parents' rebellion against God.

The text of Scripture also reveals that man is made a living being through the in-breathing of the LORD God Himself. The warm intimacy of the picture presented here for us cannot be avoided. True, the Scripture speaks in the kind of language that we would call *anthropomorphic*. This means that God is presented *in the form and manner of a human being*, although He is, always has been, and will forever be the transcendent and majestic God. With the breath of God, man comes to life in a manner that almost has the intimacy of a kiss. The second Adam, Jesus Christ, will be betrayed with the intimacy of a kiss, but He will later breath on His disciples near the dawn of the new covenant era and say, "Receive the Holy Spirit" (John 20:22).

Man is made body and soul from the beginning. The ancient Greeks taught that the soul was a divine spark trapped inside the cage of the body. Hinduism claims that the body is merely a shell, something like a candy wrapper to be discarded at death. Death, says Hinduism, is liberation from the body. Scripture reveals something quite different. The very fact that we are made body and soul from the start, prior to the fall, already implies that the redemption of man will require the resurrection of the body as an essential element of our salvation. Salvation is not an escape from the human body. Jesus Christ paid for our sins and broke the tyranny of the Devil so that we might belong to Him, body and soul (cf. Heidelberg Catechism, Lord's Day 1).

Genesis 2:7 reveals two things to us. First, mankind is clearly part of the creation itself. Both mankind and the animals are described as "living beings" (see 2:19). He, like the animals, must depend upon the vegetation of the earth for food. He breathes the air to live, and like all mammals, mankind has hair. Many more similarities could be mentioned.

But in the second place, mankind is utterly unique, according to God's Word. Only he is made in the image of God (1:26, 27). Only he has the manner of his creation described, the recipient of God's in-breathing. "Dust of the earth" cannot refer to any kind of animal ancestry because later in Genesis 3:19 we read that God says, "For you are dust, and to dust you shall return." At death, man does not revert back to being some kind of animal! Just as Genesis 1 tells us of the diversity of all creatures "in the beginning," so too Genesis 2 undercuts and refutes any and all understandings that would suggest evolutionary development of the human race.

God the Gardener (2:8, 9)

In order for man to have a place to live, the LORD God now plants and prepares a garden toward the east in the land of Eden. This is man's initial home, Paradise *par excellence*. The text mentions trees of all kinds, and then mentions two more trees. Thus the inspired narrative is allowing us to anticipate the issues that will come to prominence in Genesis 3. The trees please both the eye and the palate. Man's physical wellbeing and his aesthetic pleasure are God's concern in His every preparation for our first home. In the beginning, nothing could be better!

Rivers and rocks (2:10–14)

Genesis 2:10–14 has caused some scholars to scratch their heads: why are these verses in the Bible? What purposes do verses 10–14 serve? They almost seem to break up the flow of the narrative because verse 15 appears to pick up naturally and easily where verse 9 left off.

But in fact this description enhances our understanding of the Garden planted in the land of Eden. The river that divides into four streams suggests that Eden was on a mountain. A comparison with Ezekiel 28 seems to confirm that when it draws an analogy with the king of Tyre: "You were in Eden, the garden of God; every precious stone adorned you . . . you were on the holy mount of God" (Ezek. 28:13a, 14b). There the mountain reference is explicit. In any case, such rivers would have served to ensure the life of the plants. The Garden of Eden was well-irrigated.

Furthermore, we know at least two of these four streams (or rivers) today: the Tigris and the Euphrates. Their origins are in the Ararat mountain region of Armenia (Armenians believe that the Garden of Eden was in their land!). Is it not interesting that following the Flood, the ark carrying Noah, his family, and the creatures with him lands in a mountain in Ararat?

The river Pishon flows through the land of Havilah where there is gold, good gold. Moses' readers would have recognized in this description the fact that God made great wealth available in the beginning. In the history of God's salvation, gold plays a very important role as a means of currency as well as an important component of jewelry (hence, beauty). Abram was rich in gold (Gen. 13:2). The Syrian king Ben-Hadad received Judah's treasury of gold and silver from King Asa (I Kings 15:18). The fact that gold had high value can be seen when the Psalmist says that the LORD's judgments were more desirable than "much fine gold" (Ps. 19:10a; cf. Ps. 119:72, 127; Prov. 3:14; 8:10, 19; 16:16). John describes the city of New Jerusalem as "pure gold, like clear glass" (Rev. 21:18b). From the Garden of Eden to the eschatological (final) City of New Jerusalem (the gift of God to His own people), gold is portrayed as a very valuable and beautiful commodity. Even so, God's Word and His wisdom still exceed all the finest gold.

Work and worship

The LORD God places the man He formed in the Garden for a purpose. This place was man's home, but man has household chores to perform. Paradise was not a retirement home! It could not be that because the dominion mandate of ruling and subduing the earth (Gen. 1:26, 28) clearly implies that the man would have many tasks to perform in the creation-kingdom. Governing the Garden is an active calling.

Genesis 2:15 uses two verbs to describe man's responsibility: cultivate (i.e., work) and take care (i.e., keep, guard). The word *cultivate* means to work the earth (till the ground), but it implies far more. Cultivation of the soil means to work the ground in such a way that it brings forth the desired food but also other natural products. Development of the earth's resources for the greater glory of

God is meant. Extending the thought carries us to the entire range of cultural enterprises that make up life within the kingdom of God.

Psalm 2:11 and Psalm 100:2 use the very same verb (cultivate) to describe *service* to the LORD "Serve the LORD with gladness!" Here the reference is to the worship activities of God's people. It is striking that the same word can be used for both work and worship, for both culture and cultic activities (by *cultic* I am referring to matters of liturgy and formal worship). Reformed Christians believe with all our hearts that all of life is lived *coram Deo*, before the face of God. Abraham Kuyper reminded us that not one square inch in the whole universe of human life falls outside the kingship of Jesus Christ. Christ sees the whole, and He says, "It's mine!" Therefore, to worship the Lord on Sunday must lead to work for the Lord throughout the week.

The covenant of God's favor

The word *covenant* is not used in the Biblical text in Genesis 1–2. But we do not go far afield if we discuss the idea of covenant already at this point in the Bible. Clearly the elements of a covenant are in place here. God has taken the sovereign initiative here. He has lovingly established a relationship of friendship and favor with that one creature, man, who will rule as a vice-regent (governor) over the creation-kingdom. God loves the man, and the man must respond in love and faithfulness to his God. Man is free to eat everywhere, from all the trees of the Garden of Eden. God is not stingy with us! But there is a prohibition: the tree of the knowledge of good and evil is off-limits. Should the man cross this boundary, then death is a certainty. Man is called in this covenant of favor to believe what God has said and to glorify Him by obedience.

Points to ponder and discuss

1. What is meant by biological evolution? What is theistic evolution? What are the reasons some people believe in evolution? Does the Bible allow for (theistic) evolution? Why or why not? (Give Scriptural reasons for your answers.) Can the doctrine of creation, especially the creation of man, be isolated from other teachings of Scripture? (Think here of the doctrines of Christ, of salvation, of eschatology.)
2. What are some of the effects of an evolutionistic worldview in our society? How important is this issue today in the church, in education, in medical ethics, etc.?
3. Scripture reveals that work is good, a calling from God. How does our (North American) society view work? How might lotteries and gambling undermine the Biblical view of work? Why are some people lazy, and why are some people workaholics?
4. At one time the United States was on the gold standard to back its currency. The Eastern Roman Empire (also known as the Byzantine Empire) had gold coinage for 800 years with virtually no inflation in that period. What is it that backs up or supports the value of money today? What causes inflation and deflation? Should the government print more paper money in order to solve economic difficulties?
5. What are various Christian attitudes to involvement in culture and cultural enterprises? (Think in this regard, for example, about Roman Catholic and Anabaptist or Amish approaches to life in the world.) What is the historic Reformed view of involvement in cultural activities? Can Christians be legitimately involved as Christians in politics, the arts and entertainment, business life, the world of science, etc.?
6. God prepares the Garden of Eden as a paradise home for man. Man is put there to work for God. But then God

puts before man a test in regard to eating or not eating. Why does God do this? What do we learn about our God in these several actions of Genesis 2:4–17?

7. What do you understand by the word covenant? Is the covenant used in different senses in Scripture? Why do some Christians narrow the idea of covenant down to refer only to their children, baptism, and perhaps Christian education? Isn't covenant broader than those important things?

Lesson 7

Partners in God's Kingdom

Read Genesis 2:18–25

Very good but yet "not good"

Genesis 1:31 says that when God surveyed all that He had made, He judged that it was very good. There were no moral or spiritual flaws in His handiwork. Everything that He had created and formed fit His divine plan and heavenly blueprint. But when we come to Genesis 2:18, the LORD God declares that there is something that is "not good," namely, man's solitude. There is something lacking. This is not the discovery of a flaw, something like an artist might discover in a work of art upon its completion, for example, a chip in a statue or a smudge on a painting. Nor is this a moral lapse in the man's spiritual constitution. God is saying that man's *solitude* is something that is most undesirable. It is striking that this is God's judgment and not the man's complaint to God. Indeed, the man has not yet spoken in the record of the text. God evaluates the situation perfectly with regard to the man. Therefore, God declares that He will make a "helper suitable" for the man.

Verse 19 describes the bringing of the beasts and the birds to the man for naming. Earlier in Genesis 1 we read that the birds are God's handiwork on the fifth day while the beasts are what He created on the sixth day of the creation week. It is the tactic of some to say that the Bible contradicts itself here. In Genesis 1 the order is thus: birds, then animals, and finally man (male and female). But here the order is the following: man, then animals and birds, then the woman. But if there is a "genuine" contradiction here, it is passing strange that Moses (who wrote under divine inspiration!)

did not perceive the contradiction. The NIV translation of verse 19 ("Now the LORD God *had formed*") is a legitimate way of expressing the original language. This indicates the fact that the animal and bird worlds had already been created, and these creature realms might yield the helper suitable for Adam. Genesis 2:19 is recalling an earlier fact, and it does not necessarily mean that the animals and birds were created after the man. In other words, no contradiction between Genesis 1 and 2 can be proven at all.

Lonely or alone?

I would propose the following: man's solitude, which is declared "not good," is not primarily a reference to loneliness (in a psychical or psychological sense). Recall that the first man, Adam, had perfect fellowship and communion with God Himself. The words of Psalm 73:25, 26, would have been true for Adam as well as for a believer today: "Whom have I in heaven but Thee? And besides Thee, I desire nothing on earth. . . . God is the strength of my heart and my portion forever." In addition to covenant friendship with the LORD, Adam would have found all the creatures to be non-hostile towards him, all potential "pets" perhaps! Yet the companionship of beasts and birds for the man is not sufficient in God's grand plan.

The Jewish rabbis have a tradition that says all the animals passed by Adam in pairs. Adam saw this parade of pairs, and he then sensed his own lack. This clever spin on Genesis 2:18ff. also works with the idea that man's need of a helper suitable for him was due to loneliness. Perhaps the more important consideration about man being alone relates to his *calling*, his *office*. Adam had God as a companion, but the duties that pertained to having dominion over all the creation would be very demanding. The suitable helper for Adam would assist him in his role as king, priest, and prophet in God's creation-kingdom. She would help the man in his work of exercising dominion over the earth.

Furthermore, Adam would need another human being with whom he and she would be able to experience God's blessing in having the children that would fill the earth. Obviously Adam could not reproduce himself! God therefore takes the initiative in solving this "not good" problem.

What's a "helpmeet?"

The King James Version of the Bible in Genesis 2:18, 20, speaks of "help meet." A new word—helpmeet—was coined as a result. But what does it mean? The word for *helper* can have the idea in our language of servant, the assistant who stands in the background, perhaps the slave who has to "go for" this or "go for" that. But, in fact, the word is used many times in reference to God Himself as our heavenly Helper. Reflect on the following passages:

> Exodus 18:4: "My father's God was my helper."
> Deuteronomy 33:7: "Oh, be his help against his foes."
> Psalm 70:5: "You are my help and my deliverer."
> Psalm 121:1, 2: "Where comes my help? My help comes from LORD."
> Psalm 124:8: "Our help is in the name of the LORD, who made heaven and earth."
> Psalm 146:5: "The God of Jacob is his help."

More passages could be cited, but the general meaning of *help* and *helper* begins to become clear. The word is not pejorative, inferring a put-down for the person called a helper. The word has almost the sense of rescuer or deliverer. The helper is the one who does for me what I could not do all by myself. God said that man's calling as image-bearing ruler of the creation was such that being alone is not a good thing. Adam needed help, and none of the animals would provide this help.

The word *meet* is better translated as suitable to, a counterpart for, one who corresponds to another in a complementary way. Thus the woman will be a helper who meets Adam's need; she will, with him, help him fulfill mankind's chief end, namely, to glorify God and enjoy Him forever (cf. Westminster Shorter Catechism, Q/A 1).

The text is not saying that she is a helper *equal* to the man (the original language could have said that, but it does not say this). The study note of the *New Geneva Study Bible* for Genesis 2:18 reads thus, "The word 'helper' entails his inadequacy, not her inferiority; for elsewhere it is often used of God." This is an important point to understand in our times. The woman is not inferior in her being because of the nature of her creation. Animals are not superior because they were made first. Nor is the ground superior because man came from the ground. Male and female constitute mankind, and both are created in the image of God. But within mankind (humanity), there is a relationship, an "economy," of office-bearing. In their being image-bearers, man and woman are equally before the face of God our Father. In their respective offices, the man is the head of the woman, and "so there is a divinely imposed subordination here" (E. J. Young, *In the Beginning*, p. 77). At the same time the woman is a gift of a loving God to the man because our Lord knows that we can never make it all alone in fulfilling the divine plan for God's creation-kingdom.

Divine surgery on the man (2:21–22a)

The very specific steps that God takes to create this helper suitable for the man is to put him into a deep sleep, under a supernatural anesthetic, after which God removes one of Adam's ribs and then divinely closes (heals) the side. This deep sleep is like the sleep Abram experienced in Genesis 15:12

when God showed Himself passing between the parts of the covenant animals. The word usually translated as *rib* actually means *side*. God removed a portion of Adam's side, and so whether it was a rib in particular or something else, may be a debated point. In any case, with the "raw material" of this rib (or portion of his side) God "builds" (that is the word in the original language!) a woman. The man was described as formed from the clay by the Divine Potter, and now the Divine Builder prepares the perfect companion for Adam from the man's own body.

Read I Corinthians 11:3-16. Of special interest are verses 8, 9: "For man did not come from woman, but woman from man; neither was man created for woman, but woman for man." Paul is clearly recalling the Genesis 2 account here. At the same time Paul points out the danger of individualism and the spirit of self-centeredness when he says in I Corinthians 11:11, 12: "In the Lord, however, woman is not independent of man, nor is man independent of woman. For as woman came from man, so also man is born of woman. But everything comes form God." This should remind both men and woman of their mutual interdependence. "No man is an island." In creating the woman for the man, God is teaching the human race that we were designed to live in community and in fellowship with one another. The rugged individual may be a prized culture "hero" in some societies, but the Bible would not endorse this.

History's first wedding (2:22b–23)

Genesis 2:22b says that God "brought her to the man." If someone had been present there in the Garden for the presentation of this first bride in all of history, and had this person asked the question, "Who gives this woman to this man?" the answer would have come from God Himself, "I do. I give her to Adam to be his loving and faithful wife."

Upon the presentation of this bride, the Bible records the first human words of history in Genesis 2:23. The words come across as a kind of song, a simple hymn of praise and wonder at the gift of such a wonderful bride. They provide for her a joyful welcome into this creation-kingdom and Garden home. Truly the woman is Adam's bone and flesh (literally!). The words are used elsewhere in the Bible as a phrase to indicate kinship (see Gen. 29:14; Judg. 9:2; II Sam. 5:1). In marriage one joins another "in the Lord" so that there is a spiritual oneness. Jesus Christ must provide the common platform upon which the married couple stands. Furthermore, each married person should find in his or her spouse one's best friend and companion. There is no mention here of children (that comes in Genesis 3); the woman is prized and praised as a companion in her own right, a gift from our heavenly Father.

Marriage: what God said in the beginning (2:24)

By inspiration Moses now inserts commentary that looks ahead to that time when the human race would practice marriage. That time would come in the very next generation after our first parents. God's presentation of the woman to Adam along with Adam's recognition that God has brought the two of them together forms the context for the first explicit words of the Scripture regarding marriage. The creation of mankind—male and female—sets the original context for marriage and the home and therefore for society at large. The marital relationship existed before the fall into sin, and it becomes clear that marriage is one of the most fundamental building blocks for any sane and orderly society.

Notice what it is being set forth for marriage here in the Word of God. The man leaves his father and his mother. Of course, he must always love and respect these his parents, but the home that he is establishing and that he shall serve as its head, is a new and identifiably different unit. The marriage relationship is *exclusive*. Of course, any new husband and wife will want to have the blessing and well-wishes of their parents (if they are still living), but the man who now leaves the home of his youth does so without his parents present to direct the details of his new home and marriage. While he was under his parents, a man receives their love, instruction, protection, and encouragement. But when he leaves to marry, he now becomes responsible for this. Godly advice from one's parents is welcome, but in each marriage a new and exclusive relationship has now been established.

Secondly, the marital relationship is to be *permanent* in this life. The man is to cleave to (stay close by, bond with) his wife. The principle of one man and one wife is established in the beginning. Indeed, the nature of marriage is settled from the very beginning. While it is true that several patriarchs (Abraham, Jacob) and several kings (David, Solomon) had more than one wife, we are not to see this as normal. Consider the great troubles and difficulties that resulted because they had more than one wife! The Biblical norm for a man is to love one woman, and one woman only, in the bonds of matrimony. A great lover is not the person who loves many, many women in a lifetime, but one who can maintain his love and devotion to that one wife whom God has given him. Thus the one who would get married "forsakes" all others, and he or she becomes very circumspect to see that no one and nothing interferes or undermines the marriage relationship.

Thirdly, the marital bond is *sealed* before God through vows. The two shall be one flesh. This does not mean that the man and the woman lose their individual perspectives or respective abilities and insights. Nor does this expression have reference only to the sexual intimacy that is enjoyed in marriage. Rather, marriage is an estate into which the two enter as ordained by God, and they come together and bring together all for the sake of the other. They seal the union through promises and vows. Thus the Bible endorses marriage and a public display of commitment *before* there is the enjoyment of sexual intimacy.

Ephesians 5:22–33 expands on God's revelation in Genesis to show how the human relationship of marriage reflects the gracious relationship of Christ and His church. Christ heads the church, but He is also one with His church. He lives with His Bride. He is prepared to die for the church; in fact, He did die so that His Bride might live. In turn the church lives for Christ in loving submission and devotion. In reflection of this, wives are to submit to their husbands, showing them love and respect (cf. Col. 3:18ff.; I Pet. 3:1ff.).

Jesus was once asked by the Pharisees about the permissibility of divorce (Matt. 19:1–9; Mark 10:1–12). Jesus responds, "What did Moses command you?" (Mark 10:3). Their answer refers to a kind of permission that Moses granted in Deuteronomy 24:1–4. But the Lord reminds all of us that this particular permission was in place "because your hearts were hard." In any relationship—marriage included—after the fall into sin, sinners are involved. Even if they have the best of intentions, sinners still will have difficulties and trials in any relationship. Furthermore, the Lord points back to something that Moses wrote much earlier than Deuteronomy. Jesus quotes from Genesis 2 to indicate what God's will and intention was "at the beginning of creation" (Mark 10:6). In marriage the two are "no longer two, but one." "Therefore what God has joined together, let man not separate" (Mark 10:9).

Naked but not ashamed (2:25)

The very last words before we read of a subtle intruder are that the man and the woman are both naked, yet they experienced no shame in each other's presence. Of course it should be this way, seeing that they are innocent! Both the man and the woman are created very good, and they are thus adorned with the virtue of a godly spirit. Without sin there is no shame, no fear, no inclination to hide one's feelings, thoughts, desires, or even passions from one another.

By the end of Genesis 2 the God work of creating is complete. The thinking reader cannot help but be impressed with the fact that the Bible reveals here a God who is so completely concerned about man's well-being and happiness. No detail is left unattended until the image-bearing team is provided all that is needed to live and serve God and the development of His creation-kingdom. In Moses' day this would have sounded so wonderfully good because the deities of the Egyptians and the Mesopotamians cared very little about human welfare. Blessing rests upon the man and woman.

Yet there is a hint in the text of some "tension" in the sense that there is a tree in the middle of the Garden, the tree of the knowledge of good and evil. There is a prohibition expressed concerning it. Yet the human team must choose for the good and reject all that is evil. In so doing, they would have experience a continuing relationship of friendship, peace, and great comfort in the presence of each other, but more importantly, in the presence of their heavenly Father.

Points to ponder and discuss

1. God said that it was not good for the man to be alone. What is individualism? How is it evident in today's western society? What threats does it pose for the church, the home, and society in general?
2. What does North American society say about marriage? Or, in other words, what view or views about marriage are currently popular in our society? How do most state

governments now view marriage, and how did they view it, say, a generation ago?

3. What is feminism? Are there different versions of feminism? Why did it arise? What kind of responses can the Christian community give to feminism?
4. Read I Corinthians 11:3–12, Ephesians 5:22–33, and I Timothy 2:11–15. What does the Bible understand by headship? How has headship been abused in the past? Why does our society have such a difficult time accepting the Biblical principle of the man as head of the woman?
5. The Bible views marriage as a covenant (cf. Prov. 2:17; Mal. 2:14). What are the reasons for so many divorces today in our society? What can Christian homes, schools, and churches do to better prepare young people for marriage and the realities of home life?
6. Some Greek philosophies viewed the human body as a prison for the soul. Some Christians have treated the human body with shame and contempt. Other viewpoints allowed the body any and all indulgences. Read Matthew 10:28; Romans 6:13; 12:1; I Corinthians 6:12–20; and Philippians 1:20. What is the Biblical view of the human body?

Lesson 8

Covenant Rebellion in the Creation-Kingdom

Read Genesis 3:1–7

The first two chapters of Genesis confront us with beautiful realities about God the Creator, about the power of His Word, and His loving devotion to the crown of His handiwork, namely, mankind. There is not a hint of sin or rebellion. God left no stone unturned until everything is in place. Man is given both covenantal *privilege* as God's partner and creation's ruler but also covenantal *responsibility* as the servant and guardian of the Garden of Eden. The trees bearing fruit are all before him, and only one is expressly forbidden him, that is, the tree of the knowledge of good and evil. From that tree he may not eat for when he does, he will certainly die.

In addition, God provides the first man Adam with his wife to serve with him as covenant partners in their calling before the face of God. This causes Adam great joy, and they live before the LORD their God and before each other in happiness and profound satisfaction. But then...

Textual clues for the reader

Bible study always requires close reading in order to pick up both the broad strokes of the picture as well as the interesting and subtle clues of the inspired writer. Notice the following items. In Genesis 2:4–17 the Lord God is the active character, while man is portrayed as passive. God is busy, while man is the one created and given his calling in the Garden that God has planted. We read in verses 4–17 about "cultivating" and "guarding." We hear of the "tree of life" and "Eden."

When we move on to Genesis 2:18–25 we have more details provided. Now we read not only about the LORD God and man, but also the animals and the woman. Now certain *relationships* come into clearer focus. The man names the animals, but he also calls his wife ("bone of his bone and flesh of his flesh") a *woman*, because she was taken from the man (v. 23). Thus a fundamental headship is established by the text. There is order in God's creation-kingdom. One might call it a kind of hierarchy. It is true that the word hierarchy may have a bad connotation to many in our society today. Yet the textual givens cannot be suppressed here. Adam is the covenant head of the human race, as Paul clearly affirms in Romans 5:12–21 (cf. I Tim. 2:11ff.).

But we when come to Genesis 3:1ff., we notice that the two principal characters are the snake (a creature) and the woman. The man is "off to the side," one might say (see vs. 6–7), and the Lord God does not come back into the text in an active way until verse 8. In other words, as the text moves us closer to the center of the Garden where the trees are—and thus to the covenantal testing area—the order of the creation is "turned on its head." A lower creature, a snake (the Devil, as we shall discuss below), engages the woman in a dialogue that he controls. She falls to the temptation of the serpent, and the woman, that helper so suitable for the man, gives the forbidden fruit to the head of the covenant. They eat!

Later on in Genesis 3 we will notice how those relationships are reasserted in the text. Genesis 3:22–24 will again reveal the LORD God active and the man "passive" as he is expelled from the Garden, lest he eat from the tree of life (cf. Gen. 2:4–17).

The kingdom invaded

There is an interesting play on words in the original language (not usually caught in English translations) between the word "naked" (Gen. 2:25), describing the condition of the man and woman, and the word "crafty" (Gen. 3:1), which describes the serpent. Earlier God had told the man to keep the Garden, and that command has the added idea of guarding. Is there present here the subtle suggestion of keeping a watch out for a hostile invader, such as the evil one?

In any case, our innocent parents let down their guard as the shrewd and crafty serpent makes his approach to the woman. The reader should notice how in Genesis 3:1–5 the snake initiates the conversation, and he controls it.

But can snakes talk? There are many who scoff at this temptation account as merely myth or a fable, that is, a story written to give an account of how evil came into the world. But, many say, the odd or strange way recalled in the story has no reality in historical time and space.

The New Testament, however, clearly assumes the full historicity of this account of the temptation and fall into sin. Sin entered into the world through one man (Rom. 5:12). Through that one transgression and disobedience death has passed to all of humanity, and "the many were made sinners," resulting in the condemnation of all (Rom. 5:18, 19; I Cor. 15:20, 21).

Paul writes in II Corinthians 11:3, "But I am afraid, lest *as the serpent deceived Eve by his craftiness,* your minds should be led astray from the simplicity and purity of devotion to Christ." He notes a parallel in the kind of temptation faced by the church today with the first temptation that Eve faced. Paul even argues from both the order of creation and the order of the fall to provide a basis for his directives to the young pastor Timothy in Ephesus. Writes the Apostle Paul, "For it was Adam who was first created, and then Eve. And it was not Adam who was deceived, but the woman being quite deceived, fell into transgression" (I Tim. 2:13, 14).

Snakes do not talk. However, the shrewd and crafty creature of Genesis 3:1 is no common, creeping snake. Revelation 12:9 identifies the ancient serpent as the dragon who waged vigorous warfare against the woman (the Old Testament church) because she bore the Child who would crush the serpent's head. The serpent is the Devil (evil one) and Satan (accuser), "who deceives the whole world" (Rev. 12:9) but who is now bound for a thousand years (Rev. 20:2).

Yet Genesis 3:1 adds an important statement describing the serpent: it is a beast "that the LORD God made." The Devil is not an eternally existing deity, an evil force that always was. Nor does the Devil have all the power and might. The evil one is mighty, but only God is Almighty. Even the Devil was originally created good, but he rebelled against God and led other angels in this rebellion. The Devil may be the god of this age that many follow, but in the end all kingdoms shall become the kingdom of the Christ, and He shall reign forever and ever (Rev. 11:15).

A diabolical dialogue

The serpent speaks first, and his question suggests that God has insulted us. "Indeed, to think that God would actually say you cannot eat from every tree of the Garden?" In other words, can you really believe that God would put such unkind and unreasonable restrictions upon you? Did God really say that? The serpent comes across as very brazen, feisty, and combative. We would say that he is "picking for a fight." That is, of course, true, for the Devil is the first creature in the cosmos God created to rebel against Him. Also notice that the serpent does not begin by talking about the tree of the knowledge of good and evil. He starts with the topic in general ("any tree in the garden?"). But once he sets the topic, he has set the parameters for the discussion.

If the serpent in Genesis 3:1 seems to be ignorant ("Did God say?"), his diabolical and wicked purpose is to draw the woman out and to challenge her to join him in doubt and unbelief regarding God's Word. His trick begins to work. His poison is already entering the human system as he has succeeded in enticing her into rethinking the Word of God.

The woman responds (Gen. 3:2–3). The woman corrects what the serpent has said by referring back to God's prohibition in Genesis 2:16, 17. What is interesting to note is her paraphrasing of what God had said. She mentions "fruit" in her answer. But even more noteworthy are her words in verse 3, "You must not touch it, or you will die." The commentators are divided in their evaluation of what the woman has said. E. J. Young tends to disapprove of what the woman said, while John Calvin in general approves of her response. Aalders is probably the most accurate when he says that the woman has made the command more severe (God said nothing about not touching) while she has made the penalty for disobedience less severe (God had said, "You will *surely* die!"). How often that is true today: some Christians want to be more restrictive than God Himself, while others want to be more tolerant than God.

By engaging in this conversation that has been initiated by the serpent, the woman is "on the playing field," so to speak, that has been set by the evil one. His remarks have set the context for the discussion, and the serpent has made problematic what is not problematic. If the woman thinks that she can reason with the Devil, she is sadly mistaken. One cannot reason with evil, just as one cannot play with fire. We are told in the Bible to hate what is evil and to flee from it (cf. Amos 5:15a; I Cor. 6:18; etc.).

The serpent picks up on the last comment of the woman

(vs. 4–5). He makes a direct objection to the woman's correction. He strongly denies what she has said and what God had said. "No! You will not surely die!" In other words, God lied to you about this tree; He has not told you the truth.

Jesus once in a controversy with the Jews made reference to the Devil as a "liar and the father of lies" (John 8:44). This truth is clearly evident in his cunning deceit that he puts before the woman in Genesis 3. But Jesus says something else about the Devil: "he was a murderer from the beginning, not holding to the truth, for there is no truth in him" (John 8:44). This dimension of the temptation is sometimes overlooked. No only did the serpent "bear false witness" about what God had said, but he also was a "killer." His words led to the death of the woman and the man, indeed, to the death of the whole human race (see Rom. 5:12ff.). A wolf in sheep's clothing is still a wolf, and the wolf does not have kind and pleasant intentions for the flock. So too the serpent had murderous intentions against our first parents when he engaged in conversation with the woman. To be sure, the woman and the man were also fully responsible for what they did. They cannot say, "The Devil made me do it." They acted in the full freedom of their own will.

In this regard it is not accurate to say that the first temptation is every temptation. We are not Adam, and Adam is not Everyman. Adam was the covenant head of the whole human race, responsible before God as corporate head. Furthermore, he was created sinless, and when he sinned, he freely chose to do so. But with every one of his children, including you and me, we are conceived and born in sin. We enter this world already guilty and constituted as sinners. By nature we are prone to hate God and our neighbor (cf. Heidelberg Catechism, Lord's Day 2, Q/A 5). When we sin and fall to temptation, it is because it is our old nature to do so. Mankind's problem is not that we are humans. Mankind's problem is that we are sinners.

The anatomy of the temptation

It is important to take careful note of several things that emerge in this diabolical dialogue between the serpent and the woman. The Devil does not set out to convince the woman that God does not exist. His aim is not to make a case for atheism. Instead, he attacks the truthfulness of God's own Word. Through God's Word our Lord maintains fellowship with us, but if that Word is attacked or undermined, then soon enough the covenant bond is eroded, and friendship with God Himself first suffers and is then lost. So it is today. The Devil's first line of attack is not to turn people into those who deny God's existence. He attacks the truthfulness and infallibility of the Word of the Lord. The evil one is satisfied if he can get people to live as "functional atheists" (i.e., people who believe God exists, but it does not matter in their daily lives).

But a second teaching that comes under attack from the serpent is the doctrine of divine judgment. The Devil affirms in strong language, "You will not die!" In other words, God was lying to you about any kind of penalty for breaking His commandment regarding eating from the tree of the knowledge of good and evil. There is no death for sin, and there are no bad consequences for disobedient actions. Again, so it is today. Nearly everyone will vote to have heaven, but the percentages fall off when people are asked about the reality of God's judgment and His penalty of hell for those who are unbelievers and disobedient. Many people think, "If hell exists, it is for someone else, because I am not that bad." Someone has said somewhere that most North Americans think that the only thing one needs to do to go to heaven is to die. If you lead a "pretty good life," then God has to let you into heaven. The reality is something else: without the perfect righteousness of Jesus Christ, no one can be saved.

"Forbidden fruit always tastes sweeter," it is said. The serpent also holds out to the woman the prospect of acquiring a knowledge that will put the woman and the man (the word "you" in verse 5 is plural) on a par with God Himself. But this is not what God had said! God warned about certain death, while the serpent affirms the elevation of mankind to divine rank. In fact, the serpent is jeering God. God is keeping vital information away from the human pair. He has a secret that, if it were revealed, would actually benefit mankind. The diabolical suggestion is that this God of ours is not truly good.

To "know good and evil" is a difficult phrase to explain. God knows all things, but He certainly does not know evil experientially. The phrase suggests moral discernment, moral autonomy, the ability to be self-legislating. By taking what God has forbidden, man is violating the covenant relationship with God, and man will snatch at being divine. The tree of the knowledge of good and evil has judgment surrounding it. The woman and the man were to live in faith and obedience based on that faith in God's Word. But the evil one deliberately and in a very subtle manner cast the whole discussion into the wrong context: acquiring *knowledge* that would lead to equality with God. The question at the end of Genesis 2:17 was this: what will man do, eat (and therefore die) or not eat? But now the question at the end of Genesis 3:5 is this: whom does man believe, the snake or God? If the serpent is believed, then the covenant has been violated. If the woman and the man eat, the penalty for covenant rebellion in the creation-kingdom of God is certain death.

Eating the forbidden fruit (3:6–7)

Following the conversation between the serpent and the woman, the action now picks up speed. Her eyes are drawn to the fruit; wisdom appears to be the desired goal, if only she takes, eats, and believes the serpent.

Sin is always a matter of the heart, but it is also a matter of one's actions. The command in Genesis 2:16, 17, was not to eat. Therefore, the critical action, the operative word in Genesis 3:6, is *ate*. "She ate," and then she gave to her husband who is with her, and "he ate." Now the man is brought into the story. The man is not an innocent victim here of a trick from the woman. He is fully responsible, since he was the covenant head of the whole human race. The woman was deceived, but the man was not deceived (I Tim. 2:14). Victor Hamilton (*Genesis* 1–17, p. 191) says the following:

"The woman does not try to tempt the man. She simply gives and he takes. He neither challenges nor raises questions. The woman allows her mind and her own judgment to be her guide; the man neither approves nor rebukes. Hers is a sin of initiative. His is a sin of acquiescence."

The serpent had promised knowledge. But the result, as their eyes opened to a new reality of sin and death, is embarrassment and shame. They can no longer tolerate their own nakedness as the wonderful innocence of sinlessness is lost in one fell swoop. In a pitiful manner they now grab for the leaves of the fig to cover themselves. It will take far more to cover sinfulness: it will take the complete and flawless righteousness of a second Adam, our Lord Jesus Christ.

Points to ponder and discuss

1. Mankind had the obligation to keep and guard the Garden. Yet the tempter entered and in a subtle way took the woman down the road of temptation. What are

the steps that you (and your family) can take to guard yourself from the first steps of temptation? How easy (or hard) is this?

2. What does the Bible teach about the Devil? How seriously does our society take the existence of the Devil and the reality of the (evil) spirit realm?
3. What is understood by "free will?" During the Reformation period there was a great debate between Erasmus and Martin Luther over the question of whether man today has a free will. How would you answer that question? Support your answer from the Bible and the Reformed confessions (cf. Rom. 3:9ff.; I Cor. 2:14; Belgic Confession, articles 14–15, etc.).
4. See Matthew 4:1–11; Mark 1:12, 13; and Luke 4:1–13. What parallels, if any, can be drawn with the temptation faced by the woman in the Garden, and the temptations faced by our Lord Jesus Christ?
5. Job 1–2 records the trials of the righteous man Job. How did his situation differ from that of our first parents? Do righteous believers still face Satanic attacks today as Job faced them?
6. Read James 1:12–15 and discuss the "anatomy of temptation" as outlined by James. What is the relationship between external factors that tempt us and our own nature and inner disposition? Why do some sins tempt some people but seemingly have little effect or attraction to other people?

Lesson 9

In Wrath He Remembers Mercy (Part One)

Read Genesis 3:7–15

The serpent had promised that Adam and his wife would receive the "knowledge of good and evil." What he had not told them is that they would in fact *become evil*. They would acquire more in this deal than what they were told by the evil one. Beyond getting more knowledge, they get moral guilt and corruption. So it is with all temptations. How often we allow the lure of evil to blind our own hearts to what is in the fine print of the deal.

Trying to hide (3:7–9)

Sin brings guilt and a guilty conscience. Guilt is an objective matter: one stands before the law as one who has broken (or transgressed) that law. But a guilty conscience is a subjective thing: one has the psychological sensations of embarrassment, of wrongdoing, of unease in the presence of others. The man and the woman both ate fruit from the tree forbidden to them. This made them guilty before God and His word of prohibition, but this also had the effect of making them self-conscious of their own nakedness. Now they try to hide from each other by taking the large leaves of the fig tree to sew coverings for themselves. Now begins the long history of mutual alienation. The Garden is no longer a comfortable home. It has become instead a place where fear, insecurity, and hiding are the norm.

But in addition when the LORD God comes to the Garden to have fellowship with the human couple, they also hide from

Him among the trees. But "you cannot hide from God," says the song. He is both everywhere (omnipresent) and all-knowing (omniscient). It is interesting that God's first recorded words after the fall into sin are 1) a question and 2) directed to the man. The crafty serpent had opened his diabolical dialogue with a brazen question to the woman. Here God opens His investigation into the sinful situation with a question directed to the man, the head of the woman.

Of course, God knows where the man is. So what is the nature of the question God asks? It comes off almost as indirect accusation: "Adam, where are you?" The man is not at his task, his job. He is not fulfilling his office of ruling and having dominion over all things. The man is not developing the creation-kingdom and its potentialities. In short, when God comes calling upon His beloved image-bearers, it appears that there is "no one home." Initially then, there is no longer a voice of human joy that greets the divine voice of the Creator LORD. "Where are you?" God asks. What a stab of pain and terror must have filled the soul of the man and the woman at the sound of their Maker's voice! The Garden is about to become a courtroom.

Passing the blame (3:10–13)

The man's answer to God's question is pathetic. The man claims that he hid from God because he was naked. This is a pitiful response because it is not at all accurate. Before the man and the woman fell into sin, they were both naked. They had no shame because they had no sin. So to claim the reason for hiding from God is based upon one's body being unclothed misses the point. The problem with humanity is not that we are human! Being a creature is not in itself a sinful thing at all. We often hear it said, "I just couldn't help it. I'm only human." This kind of statement assumes that humanity is inherently sinful, including both guilt and pollution (the corruption of the human nature). But the

Bible clearly informs us that our deepest problem is not that we are human, but rather that we are *sinners*. Because of sin the wrath of God comes in all its awesome fury and strict justice. God's *wrath* must be feared, not our own bodies or any other aspect of being creatures. Our *sin* must be avoided and repudiated, not what we were created to be as image-bearers of God.

So often our fears are greeted in the Bible with the precious words of comfort: "Don't fear!" or "Don't be afraid!" But such warm words of reassurance are not heard here in Genesis 3.

When God answers Adam's statement, He asks more questions. The reader should notice that God does not simply ask (v. 11), "Have you eaten from the tree?" Instead He asks, "Have you eaten from the tree *that I commanded you not to eat from*?" The operative word is "eat" because the command focused upon not eating. Furthermore, the LORD reminds the man that the tree had God's word of prohibition surrounding it. It was the word of God that Adam had violated and transgressed. God's question drives that point home in a painful way.

Adam's response is to say that the onus of responsibility for this tragic turn of events lies upon the woman that God put with him. In other words, there are two culprits in the man's view of things: the woman ("bone of his bone") and God Himself. But God made Adam the responsible head of the human race. The man took the fruit freely and willingly; the woman did not force-feed him.

The painful effect of sin was earlier to cause the man and the woman to hide from each other as they make fig leave coverings. But now they face off against each other in God's courtroom as mutual opponents, and God too is blamed as being ultimately responsible for the evil that has invaded the creation-kingdom.

God puts a similar question to the woman in verse 13: "What is this you have done?" Like her husband, she will not face up to her own responsibility in the sinful deed. She blames the serpent as a deceiver. Misery loves company, and there is enough blame to pass around to all concerned!

The wages of sin

As was said earlier, the serpent-tempter did not tell the woman that eating the fruit that God had placed off-limits would take the human couple beyond a knowledge of good and evil to actually becoming evil. But the evil one knew that this would be the case. In addition, God was crystal clear in saying that when they ate, they would certainly die.

Consider what the tragic effects of sin are in our world, effects that are already seen in Genesis 3:

1. Guilt and a loss of innocence
2. Pollution and corruption of the human nature, including the will
3. Alienation from God and from one another
4. Accusation and the shifting of blame to everyone except oneself
5. Painful living, unpleasantness, unhappiness, disease, and all kinds of human calamities
6. Power plays and manipulation to get what one wants
7. Death, the "wages of sin," experienced in body and soul, now and forever.

You can perhaps add even more to this list. But this also suggests what the ultimate results of God's redemption and salvation will be. God's grace will, in time, overcome all sin and its ugly effects, "far as the curse found." The Triune God's grace will bring the following gifts (corresponding as a remedy to what sin has introduced):

1. Perfect innocence and complete righteousness
2. Wholeness and health in every aspect of our human nature
3. Reconciliation with God and with others
4. Forbearance and mutual acceptance
5. Peace, joy, wholesome pleasure, unspeakable happiness
6. Ability and willingness to live responsibly with others in community
7. Life, even life more abundant for His elect, as well as a renewed creation.

Sentencing the primary culprit (3:14)

The serpent entered the text first in Genesis 3:1, and he is the last to be addressed by the LORD. But the serpent, in distinction from the man and the woman, is not asked any questions. The LORD immediately launches into pronouncing sentence.

What is rather striking about the Lord's sentencing of the serpent is that God declares the evil one to be cursed above all the other animals. The ground is also cursed (see 3:17). But the technical word for *curse* is not used for the woman or for the man. All are sentenced and punished, but only the serpent and the ground are cursed.

We also note that with the serpent's, the woman's, and the man's sentencing there are two areas affected: 1) an essential life function within creation; and 2) a relationship with another being. Note the following:

1. Regarding the *serpent*:
    a. Crawling on belly with dust as its "food"
    b. His seed versus the *woman's* seed, with her Seed to crush the serpent's head

2. Regarding the *woman*:
    a. Bearing children becomes painful

   b. Her desire is toward her husband, although he should rule her

3. Regarding the *man*:
   a. Working the *ground* will become difficult toil as man seeks to get the food he needs
   b. In the end he will return to the dust (ground) from which he was made.

Sin has introduced all these painful realities and disruptions in relationships. God's words in Genesis 3:14–19 make all of this pointedly explicit.

The key words and phrases in verse 14 are *crawling* and *eating dust*. Both of them speak of humiliation, subjugation, and eventual defeat (cf. Lev. 11:42; Ps. 72:9; Isa. 49:23; 65:25; Mic. 7:17). Crawling does not presuppose that prior to this point, the serpent moved about on legs. Crawling is symbolic of craftiness and being a "low life." The evil one remains a trickster that employs his wiles to defeat God's people (cf. I Pet. 5:8). Eating dust is not a description of a snake's diet. Rather it is a Biblical idiom for death (cf. the modern expression, "bite the dust"). Dust, both here and in verse 19, reminds us of man's origin and destiny when the spirit of life departs. Dust thus becomes a symbol of death in the Biblical framework of thinking.

The "mother promise" (3:15)

In the context of cursing the serpent for what he has done in tempting the woman and the man, God reveals something of incredible significance. He promises that He will put enmity into history between two kinds of seed (i.e., people). This presupposes that the serpent and the woman were in some kind of alliance or partnership. In a very significant way they were partners in the early part of Genesis 3.

This is because the one you obey is your master. The

Apostle Paul writes, "Don't you know that when you offer yourselves to someone to obey him as slaves, you are slaves to the one whom you obey—whether you are slaves to sin, which leads to death, or to obedience, which leads to righteousness?" (Rom. 6:16). The woman and the man offered themselves to the serpent to obey his suggestive ways, and in doing so they made themselves slaves of the evil one. The alliance between the serpent and the woman, however, is not a relationship of peace and friendship. It is slavery! The evil one does not have kind intentions in mind for any human being who follows his ways.

God breaks that unholy alliance by placing or inserting enmity between two groups of people. Here we see divine initiative: God is the first to make a start. In addition to this initiative we note that it is *enmity*, hostility, division, that the LORD God is bringing to the earth and into history. This is not a pleasant prospect, for this means that history will be marked by spiritual (and other kinds of) conflict. Even our Lord Jesus Christ reminded us that He came to bring a sword to the earth and not peace (Matt. 10:34). Spiritual division spans all of history, both Old and New Testament eras.

Part of our salvation is coming to the awareness that the Devil is not our friend. He had tried to present himself as such to the woman, but the truth is that he was then, and he remains today, a most poisonous enemy and a very cruel taskmaster. The evil one was a liar and a murderer from the start. God is sentencing the serpent, while the message being conveyed to the sinful pair is that God is the true friend of sinners, including the first two sinners in history, our original parents.

This spiritual division is often called the *antithesis*. This is a spiritual separation that God installs. We are not permitted to remove this antithesis, nor may we blunt its ramifications in any area of life. A false kind of ecumenism in church life and elsewhere tugs at our hearts and conscience when we hear the cry, "Can't we *all* just get along?" But unity for Christians comes from a true spiritual unity in the faith, created by the Holy Spirit through the Gospel of our Lord Jesus Christ. All other bases of unity (racial, economic, cultural, national, etc.) fail ultimately to provide such unity.

The fact that divine judgment plays so dominant a role in this section of Genesis 3 should not cause us to miss something else that is most astonishing. We have in Genesis 3 the revelation of the covenant of grace. In disclosing His wrath against the sin of man, God is also revealing His mercy. The evil one is going down to crushing defeat! Thus mankind's willful rebellion is not the last word, and therefore, it should not receive the loudest emphasis, even here in Genesis 3.

The serpent's seed here is obviously not a reference to literal snakes. Our spiritual enemy is not the reptile! It is the evil one himself and all who are spiritually allied with him. Similarly the seed of the woman is prophetic of the coming Messiah, Jesus Christ. *He* will deliver a deathblow (striking the head) to the serpent, while in the process He Himself will be wounded (striking the heel). God and Satan will do battle via their respective agents in history, in time and space. Thus Christ is the chief agent of God, the Suffering Servant of the LORD, who enters our history, taking on our own nature, to win the cause for God our Father. Jesus Christ will do as the last Adam what the first Adam failed to do, namely, guard the Garden from crafty invaders, rebuke the tempter, and kill him. Therefore, because of what Jesus Christ would later do for us, the remarkable thing about the message of Genesis 3 is not so much that the sinner will die—God assured us of that—but that through the promised Seed there will be life!

Points to ponder and discuss

1. In Genesis 3:10 the man points to a symptom (ashamed because he was naked) but not to the real cause of his flight from God. The man appears more embarrassed that he was caught than that he willingly and knowingly broke the commandment of God. Why does this sound so familiar? Why do we so often respond in a similar way?
2. Blaming someone else has a long history, as we have seen in Genesis 3. Why is it so hard to face up to our own responsibilities in situations, especially in situations where our mistakes and sins are involved? Why is blaming-shifting especially reprehensible among our leaders in church and society?
3. Read James 4:4 and I John 2:15–17. Why is it so hard to convince people that evil will, in the end, lead to disaster and judgment? What does it mean that "friendship with the world is hatred toward God"?
4. Genesis 3:15 is known as the "mother promise" or "first gospel" (*protoevangelium*). How does this connect with the work and ministry of the Lord Jesus Christ? Does the Old Testament already proclaim a *Christian* message, or does the Old Testament's message differ significantly from that of the New Testament? See Heidelberg Catechism, Lord's Day 6, Q/A 19.
5. The word *antithesis* is not discussed very often in modern Christian circles. Do you agree? Why might this be the case? How should the antithesis show itself in the area of education? Politics? Entertainment?
6. Genesis 3:15 is a prophecy of the effective work of the Lord Jesus Christ is defeating the evil one (and all evil as well). Yet Romans 16:20 reads, "The God of peace will soon crush Satan under your feet. The grace of our Lord Jesus be with you." Read Malachi 4:1–3. What is the relationship between Christ's work of crushing Satan's head and Christian activity in history against Satan and his realm?

7. Jesus said, "Do not suppose that I have come to bring peace to the earth. I did not come to bring peace, but a sword" (see Matt. 10:34–39). It is easy perhaps to talk about the antithesis in areas of life that are somewhat distant from our daily lives. But how should the antithesis affect even dating, marriage, family life, and relationships within congregations and denominations?

Lesson 10

In Wrath He Remembers Mercy (Part Two)

Read Genesis 3:16–24

After the woman and the man ate the forbidden fruit, they became the objects of God's penetrating interrogation and then sentencing. Already in judging the serpent, God makes known to the reader (and thus to all subsequent history) that He has established a covenant of grace. In this covenant He will cause the ultimate defeat of the serpent and his seed (followers). The woman will bring forth the One in history who will crush the evil one's head. In His hatred of and wrath against sin, God shows undeserved mercy and grace. The end of history will see the victory of our God. But God has more to say in this the sentencing phase of man's trial.

The woman sentenced (3:16)

In approaching verse 16 we are coming to a text that has, admittedly, provoked much comment and discussion. The LORD God turns to her to describe first how something that belongs to the woman's nature and physical being (childbearing) is now affected by sinfulness. God says, "I will greatly increase your pains in childbearing; with pain you will give birth to children." Genesis 1:26–28 says that mankind is both male and female and is blessed in such a way that they are fruitful in order to fill the earth with other God-glorifying image-bearers. But now that grand blessing (and mandate) is carried out in a painful way. Children are God's rewards (Ps. 127:3), and some women are fruitful in bearing children (Ps. 128:3), but bearing them and raising them can sometimes cause much pain and heartache because these children are conceived and born in sin.

But God has more to say, and the last half of verse 16 typically provokes discussion about what God's Word here means. One very responsible discussion of this text may be found in Susan Foh's book, *Women and the Word of God*. The two critical words under consideration are *desire* and *rule*. The word *desire* is used in only three places in the Old Testament (Gen. 3:16b; 4:7b; and Song of Sol. 7:10). This word in English suggests sexual urging, and that is plausible at a first reading of Genesis 3:16. Song of Solomon 7:10 would support a sexual understanding.

However, the usage of *desire* in Genesis 4:7b is clearly not sexual. Furthermore, a related word in Arabic has the sense of "to urge, drive on" but not in a sexual way. In fact, human experience shows that sexual desire is generally more easily aroused among men than it is among women. So understanding the woman's *desire* in Genesis 3:16b as sexual is open to serious question.

Comparing Genesis 3:16b with 4:7b (comparing Scripture with Scripture) shows that similar phraseology is being used in both passages. In the case of Cain, sin is crouching at the door, and it *desires* to have him. But in what sense? Certainly not sexually! Rather, sin wants to master him, to dominate him, to control him. Cain would have to wrestle with sin to overcome it. In other words, he *should* rule it. But in fact he does not rule over sin.

The woman too will want to master the man (*desire* in the sense to wish to have control), but instead he *should* rule her. The word *rule* here is related to the word used to describe what the sun and moon do with the day and the night, respectively. That is to say, the word *rule* need not at all have a negative meaning. It does not mean to domineer as a tyrant. Mastery or lordship is not inherently evil.

In other words, God is here reasserting the Biblical relationship of man's headship (he is created first, he identifies her as *woman*, he is the covenant head of the human race) with respect to the woman He gave the man. But in her sinful condition she will desire to make herself the head or ruler in this relationship. It is not what God has created that has led to the "battle of the sexes." Rather, our sinful rebellion and fallen natures has led to such sad conflicts.

Groaning ground, sweat, and dust (3:17–18)

Genesis 3:17–19 records the LORD God's judgment on Adam, the head of the human race. God repeats a lengthy statement of his sin (the charges before the Judge and the court): the man had listened to his wife and ate from the tree concerning which God had commanded that he not eat. He was called upon to be the head of his wife, but instead, he submitted to her sinful lead.

Furthermore, the ground is now said to be cursed. The peaceful connection that had existed between the human couple and the ground (all creation is implied) is characterized by divine judgment and curse. If blessing suggests fruitfulness and productivity, then curse brings barrenness and a difficult struggle to bring forth food and everything else that is useful from God's creation. Where God's curse exists, then death must come eventually. The disobedience at this one tree, that of the knowledge of good and evil, has now brought evil and disaster. This is felt in painfully personal but also in cosmic ways (Rom. 8:16ff.).

Man's work becomes painful toil in order to obtain food. Bringing forth life and support for life are hard. Thorns and thistles will grow in the presence of the man. Fulfilling his calling and his office in this old creation now becomes painfully difficult. Through labor that brings forth his sweat he may yet eat in order to sustain his physical life, but in the end he still dies and returns to the dust from which he is made. The beasts will also die, and man dies like the beast, and yet with a difference (see Ps. 49). When the man and the woman ate the forbidden fruit, they died spiritually, and their bodies began the process of dying. God was not lying in His warning!

The woman's new name (3:20)

At the end of Genesis 2 the man had rejoiced at the LORD God's presentation of the suitable woman made from his side (rib). He called her "woman" because she was taken from "man." But woman is still not a personal name as such. Now in Genesis 3:20 the man names her Eve.

We should see this as a bright spot in an account that is otherwise very sobering in its depiction of human rebellion and God's divine judgment. When God had come into the Garden to seek the human couple, they had hid. When God asked His questions during the prosecution of the trial, if you will, the man and the woman had acted by blaming everyone else. Adam had accused the woman (and God, who gave her!) of being at fault. But here all that interpersonal enmity, blame-shifting, and mutual accusation give way to naming. Adam calls her "Eve" (she who gives life), because she is the mother of all the living (in the original language, the name Eve is related to a word meaning "life, living"). Genesis 2:24 viewed the woman as *wife*, while Genesis 3:20 sees the woman as mother.

This verse anticipates Genesis 4:1, where Adam and Eve will have children. But it also looks back to the gracious promise of God in Genesis 3:15, where God said that the woman would bring forth seed (children, descendants). There will be death and a return to the dust, it is true, but Adam is acting in faith in giving her this particular name. He is laying hold of God's Word of promise. The victory over the serpent and over the sin that has now poisoned all, will result in life ultimately and not death. Therefore, the woman's name must fit her office in redemptive history. Adam was covenant head who was responsible for the fall of the whole human race, but it is through the woman that the life-giving Savior would come.

Sin, as we have already observed, both alienates and isolates, but at this point in the Biblical account, we are greatly encouraged to see that God's promise of seed has enabled Adam to receive his wife back to himself again. Their marriage had been strained, but there will be no divorce here.

God the clothes-maker (3:21)

The man and woman had earlier created clothing from the fig leaves of the Garden. These would hardly last, to say the least! They could never serve to provide adequate covering of their sinful nature before the all-seeing and all-knowing God. So in another act of divine mercy the Lord God provides the human couple with a set of clothes, animal skins, so that they could exist in community with each other, but more importantly so that they could exist before God. God in His holiness cannot look upon sinners, and He will not allow sinful nature to have exposure in His presence. Thus Adam and Eve are now properly "vested" before the Lord.

Adam had been given the office of priest in the Garden in the sense that he had permission to come close to God and minister to Him. Adam was always to offer his own life and service in devotion to God. But later on in redemptive history, God would separate one man and his family, namely, Aaron, to serve as priests. The priests too would receive very detailed instructions in the proper vestments and clothing to wear when conducting their official duties. The high priest would later wear "glory-garments" that would cover him from head to toe so that he could minister in the tabernacle and the Temple, and especially in the Most Holy Place, once a year on the Day of Atonement.

Perhaps we run the danger of pressing this too hard, but is it not possible to hear already here a sound, however faint, of something that anticipates the outline of the fuller Gospel message? By killing an animal to prepare clothing for Adam and Eve, we see that these two sinners are 1) covered by something alien to them, 2) the clothing is derived from the shedding of blood, and 3) it is the result of God's action, not the action of the sinner. The Lord Jesus Christ was not an afterthought in God's grand plan of salvation. He is indeed the Lamb of God, slain to take away the sins of the world, "slain from the creation of the world" (Rev. 13:8; cf. I Pet. 1:20).

Eviction from the Garden-home . . . and into history (3:22–24)

The guilty pair is soon driven out, evicted from our original home, but not until a certain divine deliberation has occurred. In the original language verse 22 is grammatically incomplete (the NIV has smoothed out the expression). Just as we heard in Genesis 1:26–27 a divine consultation regarding man's creation, so now we hear another divine consultation about what to do with the rebellious couple.

God realizes that the snake's promise was true, in part. Now the man knows both good and evil (like God, although God is absolutely not evil in any sense of the word). God is profoundly concerned that the man might now reach out for the tree of life. Should he eat from it now, it would have only prolonged his physical existence, but it would not atone for his sin. It would not be able to provide salvation in the fullest sense of the term. Mere existence is not life, nor is it communion with the living God. To continue existing in a state of sin would be everlasting misery. God, *in His rich mercy*, bars the way to the tree of life by expelling the man and his wife out of the Garden of Eden. The way to everlasting life will be through

God's plan, not through man's efforts and his own work. Salvation is of the LORD!

The unifying theme of this last portion of Genesis 3 is the expulsion of man. While he was made from the material of the earth, yet he is now homeless following the expulsion. He is no longer at ease, not at the intended "center," but now Adam and Eve are "off-center," in misery and in "dis-ease." This perfect Garden-temple-home that God made is now cleansed of all unclean and evil personnel. Who now may ascend the hill of the LORD? See Psalms 15 and 24.

Heavenly guards to the tree of life (3:24)

Genesis 3:24 introduces the reader to *cherubim* (a plural word for *cherub*). The word cherub has come to mean in today's parlance those pudgy, winged infants that grace many paintings from the Middle Ages. Such pictures and images have made their way into many a modern-day Christmas card and thus into popular Christian imagination. But were medieval artists correct in what they painted? Was the Garden of Eden and the tree of life guarded by sweet-looking, pudgy, winged infants?

Read Ezekiel 1:4–28 and Ezekiel 10. These two passages give a much fuller description of what cherubim are like. A cherub has four faces (Ezek. 1:10; 10:14): that of a man, lion, ox, and eagle, the great creatures who rule in creation. Cherubim have four wings (the seraphim of Isaiah 6 have six wings!), and they move at the speed of lightning (Ezek. 1:14). When the cherubim fly, they create an awesome sound (Ezek. 1:24; 10:5). There are wheels associated with these cherubim, giving additional mobility to the heavenly throne they bear, and these wheels are full of eyes, representative of divine knowledge (Ezek. 1:18; 10:12). Ezekiel sees in his vision of God that above these cherubim is a sparkling, crystal-clear expanse (or pavement). Above that is the throne of heaven (Ezek. 1:26;

10:1). One like a Man is seated upon it (see Isaiah 6:1ff.; Dan. 7:13ff.). Such a description takes us some distance away from thinking of little, winged children!

Later on in redemptive history cherubim were placed in the Temple. Just within the veil that separated the Most Holy Place from the Holy Place, two large cherubim were situated. In addition cherubim were placed upon the Mercy Seat of the Ark of the Covenant, their wings stretched toward each other. Cherubim designs were on the veil of the Temple. All of this symbolized to Israel later that we cannot approach the throne of God on our own terms or in any casual way. God's throne has sentinels to keep all sinners away from His glorious majesty and holiness.

But there is more here. Man is driven out the front gate of the Garden, one might say, toward the east for it is at the east side that the cherubim are placed with their flaming sword. The Temple later would have its front door or courts toward the east. The first Garden of Eden had the precious tree of life. The Temple had a lampstand (a menorah), shaped like a tree, along with the table of showbread (food). The artwork of the Temple (palm trees, lions, cherubim) suggested to any observer the Garden, our first home. The Garden of Eden required from the very beginning faith and obedience, holiness and avoidance of all sin. The Temple required the very same from all its personnel and worshipers in attendance. Note these parallels.

In the fullness of time a second Adam came to this Temple (Luke 2:41ff.). But its personnel would reject Him. They took Him outside the city of God, Jerusalem, and they crucified Him. But when He died, the veil (with its cherubim designs) was torn from top to bottom. Now the children of Adam's fallen race may have access to the divine throne of grace. The Old Testament's mercy seat is now located in heaven where it still is a mercy seat (a throne of grace; see Heb. 4:16). The cherubim now must stand aside as sinners come forward with boldness to this throne to seek help and grace in time of need. How vast the benefits divine which we in Christ, the second Adam, possess!

The tree of life is also located in the new creation (see Rev. 2:7; 22:2, 14, 19). But our access to it must travel to a "tree" of another sort on Calvary's hill, where Christ died under the wrath of God and the sentence of a Roman governor. This makes the cross of Jesus Christ another "tree of life" for God's elect. The food available there—Christ's body and blood—is real food and drink. Whoever believes in the Lord Jesus Christ, will live forever in the Garden of God that is in the Paradise He is even now preparing for all who love His appearing. Through Jesus Christ there is a Way back home (John 14:1–6)!

Points to ponder and discuss

1. When couples marry, the groom and the bride often vow "to love and to cherish" one another, but often it turns out to be a relationship of manipulation and domination. Some husbands are tyrants (rule with cruelty), or they are absent (emotionally uninvolved, physically "too busy"). How can Christians present the Biblical teaching on male headship in a winsome, convincing way, given the situations we see in society today?
2. Man was sentenced to work by the "sweat of his brow." Yet today in North America one can work in the comfort of air-conditioned offices, homes, even tractors, utilizing many elements of technology to make life in general and work in particular, much easier. Do people in our North American context still work by the "sweat of their brow?" If so, how? What does this mean today?
3. Work was originally a blessed calling, but now we encounter "thistles and thorns," making our efforts

difficult. Yet work by individuals and by communities of peoples (employing a division of labor) has produced much more leisure time and more leisure goods in many parts of the world. Is this a good thing, a bad thing, or a mixed blessing? Explain your answer (remembering that man's nature as a sinner is still in evidence).

4. Eve is the "mother of all the living" because God fully intends to work out His covenant of grace. In the Jewish Passover the mother in the home is to light the first candle and to offer the first prayer because through the woman will come the Messiah, the "light of the world," say the Jews. In the history recorded in the Bible, what other women gave birth to very important people of the covenant? How many women in the Bible are initially barren, but then they give birth through the power of the Lord?
5. Read Galatians 3:27. What does it mean that in baptism we become clothed with the Lord Jesus Christ?
6. If cherubim are these awesome creatures as described by Ezekiel, what then are angels in the Bible? Who is that figure in the Old Testament known as the "Angel of the LORD?"
7. The tree of life has a long history in redemption history, even though it is mentioned relatively little. Yet it appears at the beginning of the Bible in Genesis and then again at the end in Revelation. It provides food for those who persevere and conquer now. What kinds of Biblical connections can we make between the Person and work of the Lord Jesus Christ, the Lord's Supper, the tree of life in Paradise (Rev. 2:7; 22:2, 14, 19), and the Messianic banquet yet to come?

Lesson 11

Degeneration in the Generations

Read Genesis 4

As part of the punishment of the LORD God, expulsion from the Garden of Eden is the result of Adam and Eve's rebellion. But in the judgment of God, there will be a "seed of the woman" that will crush the serpent's head. Divine wrath came upon the human race in Genesis 3 but not without divine mercy. God reveals the covenant of grace.

The first family (4:1–2a)

The "mother promise" of Genesis 3:15 spoke of seed to come, i.e., children, descendants. Here we observe that God's original intentions expressed in Genesis 1:26–28 are not frustrated. Mankind, under God's blessing, is to be fruitful, multiply, and fill the earth. Mankind is called to rule and have dominion over all the earth, to till and keep this world for God's glory. Genesis 4 will now show that mankind, even in the state of total depravity and corruption still can produce, both children and products from the creation.

Adam had not rejected his wife in Genesis 3, but he took her to himself and named her Eve, "mother of the living." He loves her again, and he "knew" her. In knowing Eve in a close, intimate way, Adam has a son, but the text focuses on Eve as mother of a son, even the one who names the son. She calls the first baby of human history *Cain*, a name that sounds like the word meaning "acquired" or "obtained." "With the help of the LORD I have brought forth (acquired) a man," she says.

The events of Genesis 4 must be read on the background of Genesis 3:15 and 3:20. This in part helps us understand what motivates Eve's naming of Cain. A son is born, and she may wonder, "Is this one the promised seed from the Lord who will crush the serpent's head?" We the readers know that Cain is not the one, but Eve may very well have hoped for this in the birth of Cain. The name of Cain suggests hope for victory.

By contrast the name of the second son, *Abel*, is not so hopeful. Abel means "breath," "meaningless," even "vanity" (cf. Eccl. 1:2; 12:8). Perhaps he was weak and sickly at birth so that his parents were discouraged about any longevity of life. After all, sin leads to death, and man, being made of dust, will return to dust in death.

Deception and murder (4:2b–8)

The text reveals that both of these two sons of Adam and Eve are productive in work. This underscores the fact that God's judgment does not undo our humanity, nor does sin cancel our responsibility and calling before God. In fact, curiosity about the world around us and exploring that world, is so much a part of human nature that it is done almost instinctively. It is almost like the normal two-year old child who is so quick to explore the world around him or her, to touch things, and to get into the surrounding environment. Work is integral to our humanity, but work is to be done for the glory of God and the wellbeing of our neighbor.

Abel was a keeper of livestock, while his older brother Cain worked the soil (cf. 2:15). There is nothing inherently wrong with either calling; both kinds of work exercise a kind of dominion over creation.

We may believe that Adam and Eve knew and taught their children some of the basics of the worship of God. These basics include that fact that we are required to present ourselves before God with humble and contrite hearts, and we must come before the LORD with gifts and not empty-handed. These principles became part of the Law that God gave to Israel in the Wilderness (see Exodus 13:2, 12; Lev. 3:14–16; Deut. 16:16). The firstborn among the people and the livestock belonged to the LORD. The best portions (the "fat") of the sacrificial animal also must be offered to God.

Cain's practice was to offer some of the ground's produce. Produce could be presented to the LORD later according to Deuteronomy 26:1–11, but we should note that this is a bloodless offering. The shedding of blood is necessary for the forgiveness of sins (see Heb. 9:22). Any kind of offering, any kind of "religious activity," any kind of human endeavor that does not take into account the need of blood sacrifice for making atonement, is an attempt to bribe God and gain merit with Him. God sets the standards for how we may become right with Him. We may never offer to God worship that we think is right and that is done to please us, first of all.

Sometimes this question is debated in the case of Cain and Abel's worship: was the Lord God's attitude of pleasure and displeasure directed toward them (i.e., their heart attitude), *or* was it directed toward their particular offering? This is a false dilemma. "The LORD looked with favor on Abel and his offering" (4:4b). Both elements, the person and his offering, are mentioned. The New Testament confirms this. Hebrews 11:4 says that Abel offered what he did "by faith" when he gave God the fat portions of the firstborn animals. Conversely, I John 3:12 says that Cain was of the evil one, hating his brother to such a degree that he killed him. He did not see that he needed to offer up to God the best, the blood, and certainly his heart.

When Cain notices the LORD's pleasure toward Abel and his offering, Cain is visibly angry. How hard it is to keep what is inside from eventually showing on the outside! His anger is directed against Abel, but in fact Cain is angry with God. It is God who determines how He is to be approached, worshiped, and adored. That is not for us to determine! Cain should have investigated that which would please God and then humbled himself. God even confronts Cain with a diagnosis of his great spiritual danger. Sin, like a lion, is crouching at the door, ready to devour him! God gives Cain time and space to repent. But instead, like the serpent before him, Cain deceives his brother into thinking it is safe (a lie!). They go to the field together where Cain commits murder against his own godly brother. How the wicked hate the righteous, even today!

Divine judgment . . . again! (4:9–16)

There are more parallels with Genesis 3. Just as God came to the Garden earlier with the question, "Where?" (cf. Gen. 3:9), so now He comes to ask Cain as well, "Where is your brother Abel?" Cain's answer is a bold, icy-cold lie: "I don't know, and I don't care!" How different later on David's confession would be when he is confronted with his adultery and murder. We wonder just how degenerate a person like Cain could be so early in human history.

Abel's innocent blood cries out for justice from the soil that has been polluted by murder. God hears the cry of the blood, and He will repay "life for life." Yet God's punishment shows both justice and mercy. Cain is cursed in his soul, made a wanderer in his body, and he becomes unfruitful in his labor. Then, and only then, does he throw himself upon the mercy of the court, because he fears for his own life (the danger coming from other descendants of Adam who would act now as "avengers;" cf. Num. 35:12ff.). God puts a mark on Cain (unknown to us as to what it was) that serves as a sign to everyone that this judged man is still protected from human execution. Yet this section ends on a very chilling note: "So Cain went out from the LORD's presence." The physical departure seems to symbolize what has been true in his own soul.

From Cain to Lamech (4:17–24)

Genesis 4:17 is similar to 4:1 and 4:25 in that all three verses tell us that children are born to several important characters in this chapter: Adam, Cain, and then Adam again. The son born to Cain is Enoch (not to be confused with another Enoch in Gen. 5:19–24). Cain now builds a city, thus repudiating God's judgment of wandering on the earth. Furthermore, Cain demonstrates his pride by naming this city after his own son. Thus Cain will have seed after him, and that son will have an abiding physical "monument" to carry his name.

Of the next generations after Enoch, we know nothing more than their names: Irad, then Mehujael, then Methushael, and finally Lamech. From Adam to Lamech inclusive, there are seven generations. Occasionally, commentaries will point to the frequent usage of seven (or its multiples) in this chapter (e.g., 4:15, 24). Seven is a number that often refers to completion, even perfection. A complete week has seven days, for example. By the seventh generation of mankind, we arrive in the text at a man who is a bigamist and a braggart. Such is the progress of degeneration caused by sin in the heart of man throughout every generation.

Lamech takes two wives (4:19), acting contrary to the principle of one man, one wife, in Genesis 2:24. The more wives one has, obviously the more children one can have. Lamech has children that are important people culturally. The Bible describes Jabal, Jubal, and Tubal-Cain as the "fathers of" agriculture, of the arts, and of industry. Even today we might say that Marconi was the "father of" the radio. Lamech's children are cultural "movers and shakers," one might say. Civilization made great "progress" under the influence of Lamech's children. But they grew up in the home of a man whose worldview and morality stand diametrically opposed to the kingdom of God.

Trumpeting one's revenge

The speech of Lamech (4:23–24) is sometimes called the "Song of the Sword." In these words Lamech boasts of how he took the life of young man who had wounded him. Furthermore, he declares that the quantity of personal revenge that he seeks far outstrips the vengeance to which Cain was entitled. He goes beyond the Biblical principle of an "eye for an eye." Lamech demands the death penalty because someone only hurt him.

The "Song of the Sword" thus celebrates a boastful brutality that runs counter to the law of God (see Deut. 32:35) and counter to the "milk of human kindness." Yet the song describes for us, in stark terms, the kind of depravity and revenge-seeking that is so common in history, even up until recent times. The end of the 20th century has witnessed horrific atrocities in the Balkins, the Middle East, Northern Ireland, Rwanda, and elsewhere.

Serpent seed in human flesh

The plain and painful reality of this chapter's revelation is to explain more clearly what the natures of the woman's seed and the serpent's seed are (recalling Gen. 3:15). Obviously, "serpent's seed" does not mean that there will be a long line of literal snakes that constitute God's and man's enemies. By *nature* the woman produces in her children "serpent seed." Adam and Eve's children are people who become jealous and bitter, who hate, who deceive, and who kill. Even then there is little remorse. And this callousness is already evident by the second generation of the human race! The second generation of mankind is stubborn and rebellious, willing to resist God the Creator-King. *By nature*

Adam and Eve produce children physically who are spiritually prone to hate God and their neighbor. Thus, in effect, they remain in fellowship with the evil one, the Devil. The antithesis (spiritual enmity) displays itself within the body of the human race.

Here exists the dilemma faced by humanity in Genesis 4 and also in our own day: how can there be this "seed of the woman" if *by nature* we produce "serpent seed?" The seed of the woman comes by sovereign grace alone. Remember that it was the LORD God who said, "*I* will place enmity." In this life we never have the ability to see anyone's heart, but we can see the fruit of what lives in the heart. One can tell who is part of the seed of the woman when a person or persons acknowledge and then live according to the *enmity*, the spiritual division, that God has instituted by grace. Through redemptive history, the seed of the woman is that body of people who, by sovereign grace alone, hate evil and its instigator and chief proponent, the Satan. The one Seed who will do battle against the Satan is the Lord Jesus Christ. He is the One who crushes the serpent's head.

Therefore, as we have indicated in earlier lessons, the covenant that now is absolutely central after the sinful rebellion of our first parents, Adam and Eve, is the *covenant of grace.* That one, critical covenant, to be sure, will be worked out in historically established covenants with Noah, with Abraham, with all Israel under Moses, with Phinehas (Num. 25:12, 13), and with David. Each one of those covenants in history has its own particular place, persons, promises, requirements, and emphases. But the phrase, "covenant of grace," reminds us of two things: *covenant* points out the historical character of God's dealings with a particular people in time and space, while the word *grace* points out that God has shown us undeserved mercy. Something miraculous and supernatural must happen in this creation so that God's mercy, according to His sovereign decree, will create a people "who call upon the name of the LORD" (4:26). Without the gracious kingdom of God controlling ultimately the course of events, the end result would be a world filled with people who are technologically civilized yet increasingly more brutal.

Hope placed in another seed (4:25–26)

Genesis 4 is an "epilogue of shame" to the "generation of the heavens and the earth" (Gen. 2:4). Sinfulness corrupts absolutely the human race in its standing before Almighty God. Building cities and accomplishing great cultural things may make life more comfortable, but nothing that any human can do will make mankind better or more righteous.

Yet this chapter ends on a hopeful note. The text has taken the story of sinful Cain to its terrifying endpoint in the person of boastful Lamech, but then it goes back to Adam again. Here again we see a literary "flashback" so that the reader is made to reach back to an earlier place in time and then move forward again with another line of characters.

Because of God's gracious purposes in Christ Jesus, there is more to be said than seeing how sinfulness corrupts us in ever increasing measure. Adam again knew (loved, became intimate with) Eve his wife. They had a third son. His name is again significant and meaningful. *Seth* comes from a word meaning "to place, to set, to grant." Cain was not the promised conqueror of the evil one, and Abel is dead. But through one man, the covenant line can move ahead into history, by God's grace. Seth's son is Enosh, meaning "man."

The text ends on a ray of light when it tells us that at that time men "began to call upon the name of the LORD." This family practiced a simple kind of public worship of the true God, and this pleases God. No great cultural achievements are mentioned in this family line. Yet it is in the hearts of the humble and the contrite that God is pleased to dwell (cf. Isa. 66:2). Thus the ray of light at the end of Genesis 4 comes from the "seed of the woman," Jesus Christ, who would descend from Seth and Enosh. In all the degeneration evident here, the kingdom of God is not at all crushed. Hope seemed to die with Abel's death and Cain's punishment, but hope was resurrected with the birth of and in the line of Seth.

Points to ponder and discuss

1. Both Cain and Abel brought offerings before the LORD but the LORD had consideration or favor for only one worshiper and his offering. How important is worship for Christians today? What kind of worshiper and what kind of worship please the LORD?
2. In Genesis 4:10 the LORD says to Cain, "Your brother's blood cries out to Me from the ground." Read Luke 11:50–51; Hebrews 11:4; and Hebrews 12:24. For what did Abel's cry out? What does the sprinkled blood of Jesus the Mediator say to us today?
3. Cain built a city, thus going against God's sentence of wandering. The city suggests to us today civilization and protection. But by concentrating people together, sinners are also concentrated together. What of good and evil does the Bible say about "the city?" What constitutes true community? What should the attitude of the church and of Christians be toward cities today? What is the Christian mission to the cities of the world?
4. Read Matthew 5:21–26; Ephesians 4:26, 27; and James 1:19–21. Is anger ever justified for a Christian? If so, under what circumstances? Cf. Heidelberg Catechism, Lord's Day 40, and Westminster Larger Catechism Q/A 134–136.
5. What is meant by "total depravity?" What is meant by "total inability?" Is it appropriate for Christians to

speak of themselves—regenerated and converted—as still "totally depraved?" Why or why not?

6. Read Matthew 18:21–35. Peter asks if forgiveness should be extended seven times to a brother who sins against him. But Jesus commends showing forgiveness "seventy seven times" (or, "seventy times seven," according to some translations). What is an easier course to pursue—seeking revenge or showing forgiveness? Why? What factors are necessary in showing forgiveness?
7. The 20th century has seen two horrible world wars. Where did these wars start—in remote Third World countries or in civilized Europe? What factors explain the brutality of war in these "civilized," modern times and places?

March 3rd

Lesson 12

Death's Reign from Adam to Noah

Read Genesis 5:1–6:8; Romans 5:12–21

The account ("generations") of the heavens and the earth covered Genesis 2:4–4:26. It recorded God's perfect creation and His placing there of a perfect working team (our first parents). But within this account we read of our sinful rebellion against God, a rebellion that is met with both punishment as well as the revelation of the covenant of grace in the "seed of the woman" (Gen. 3:15). The "epilogue of shame" in Genesis 4 tells a sordid tale of bitterness, deception, murder, and boastful vengeance, even as civilization takes several leaps forward. Only in the covenant line of Seth is there a ray of hope.

Made in Adam's image (5:1–5)

Genesis 5 opens the second major account ("generations"), but the focus is now on Adam and what became of his line. Genesis 5:1–5 provides both a summary and a contrast. As a summary, it reminds the reader that God made mankind originally in His image (Gen. 1:26–28). This was an image of perfect righteousness and holiness as well as true knowledge. Mankind was created male and female, receiving the blessing of God, which would enable them to be fruitful, to multiply, to fill the earth, and to have dominion over all the creatures in God's creation-kingdom.

But this passage also confronts us with a contrast, one that arises because there has been a rebellion. Man is now constituted a sinner, guilty with regard to God's perfect holiness and will, and corrupt in his very nature. By Genesis 5 this is what Adam's image is, clearly differ from what God's image is. Therefore, it is really quite sobering to read that Adam "had a son in his own likeness, in his own image" (5:3). Though Seth is the son in whom the covenant line would be continued, that same son Seth is a sinner, conceived and born in Adam's sin (cf. Ps. 51:5).

"So death spread to all men" (5:6–31)

Reading this passage at family devotions can sometimes be for us rather tedious because of the names that are hard to pronounce, names of men of whom we know so little. The Scripture at this point follows a very deliberate pattern. Notice that there are ten generations listed from Adam to Noah. After the Flood there will be ten generations listed that will take us to Abraham. Also, just as the genealogy of Cain in Genesis 4 ended with an important character with three sons (Lamech's sons in 4:20–22; cf. Adam's three sons), so too Genesis 5 ends with Noah and mention of his three sons (5:32). The Biblical text gives more attention to these noteworthy figures.

The men listed in the genealogy each takes up three verses, and again the Scripture follows a deliberate pattern: X lived so many years, and begot Y. After the birth of Y, X lives so many more years, and he has other children. X lived so many years, "and then he died."

This genealogy thus does two things for us. On the one hand, we see the continuity in the human race, specifically in the covenant line of Adam through Seth. Life is continued by the sheer mercy of God. On the other hand, the refrain, "and then he died," reminds us that what God had warned in Genesis 2:17 and confirmed in 3:19, is absolutely true. Mankind is now made mortal, not because we are made of dust, but mankind is mortal because he is a sinner. "The wages of sin is death," says the Apostle Paul in

Romans 6:23. Despite the long lives of all these men recorded in this genealogy, some living almost a millennium, nevertheless each of them came to that moment when God called him out of this life. Death spread throughout each generation and down through all the generations.

Paul takes up this point in some detail in Romans 5:12–21. He shows the contrast in how two covenantal heads effect all those within their respective covenants. Adam was the covenantal head of the entire human race. Through one man, sin entered the world, and it permeated the entire human race. "In Adam's fall, we sinned all." The consequence is that death accompanied the presence of sin. Thus every human being becomes subject to the consequence of sin, namely, death. In fact, Romans 5:13, 14 says that death reigned even over those who did not sin as Adam had sinned.

Adam was, however, a type (or pattern) of the One to come, namely, Christ. By His righteous act (Rom. 5:18), Christ secured righteousness that brings life for all within the covenant of grace. Those in Christ, though they die physically, are constituted righteous, no longer subject to condemnation (Rom. 8:1). It is only through God's sovereign grace, given freely in Jesus Christ, that the depraved and dying members of Adam's race receive the gift of righteousness, and thus they live.

Another seventh from Adam: Enoch (5:18–24)

Genesis 4 tells readers about the braggart and bigamist Lamech, the 7th person from Adam through Cain. But the 7th person recorded from Adam through Seth is the man Enoch, the father of Methuselah. The time that Enoch was on this earth was only (!) 365 years, while his son lived the longest life recorded in the Bible: 969 years.

Since Enoch's length of life is considerably shorter than that of his ancestors, the Biblical text takes time to explain. Yet what it says is tantalizingly brief. "Enoch walked with God; and he was not (he was no more); for God took him" (5:24).

During the intertestamental period, many legends arose among the Jews about Enoch. The legends say that he was shown all the secrets and mysteries of heaven, he was knowledgeable in the sciences of mathematics, astronomy, and calendars. Modern Jewish interpretation (e.g., Nahum Sarna, *Genesis*, JPS Torah Commentary, p. 43) says that the phraseology used to describe Enoch's departure is actually a nicer way to say that God took his life away prematurely in a sudden, unexpected, and unexplained way. Sarna's commentary points to Ezekiel 24:16, 18 and Jonah 4:3 for support (e.g., Jonah asks God to take his life away).

But the New Testament makes clear what the Old Testament says implicitly. Hebrews 11:5, 6 says that the reason Enoch could not be found was that God took him and that "he did not experience death." Before God took Enoch away from this life, Enoch pleased God by believing God *in this life.*

Enoch's life and Lamech's life (discussed in the last lesson) stand in sharp contrast to each other. Lamech boasted of his revenge and his violence. Enoch, on the other hand, has no speeches recorded. The text adds to the picture that he not only lived, but, most significantly, he "walked with God," and this fact is repeated twice (5:22, 24). We learn *how he lived.* The relative brevity of his life should not be seen as any kind of punishment for a specific sin of his. The same phrase is used in Genesis 6:9 to describe the man Noah. Malachi 2:6, in describing God's intentions for the priest, the one who served in the very presence of God, says that the priest (Levi) walked with God in peace and uprightness.

This walk of life was a life of faith and obedience. We are not told how much explicit detail concerning God's will that Enoch knew. Yet Enoch took personal hold of the revelation of God Himself and of His will, he believed in the true God, and his life reflected a commitment to God's way. By grace through faith Enoch enjoyed in this life in a small way something of the rich fellowship with God that Adam once enjoyed in the Garden.

In addition, Jude 14, 15 informs us that Enoch prophesied concerning the Lord's judgment against the ungodly, both what they said and what they did that was ungodly. Like righteous Abel before him, Enoch could not have been popular for his witness to God's righteousness and against the current sin in the human race. Perhaps God took Enoch out of this life to remove him from the increasing degeneration caused by people who embodied Lamech's cruel spirit and worldview. In any case, Christians who today walk with God by grace through faith may look with eagerness to experiencing some day what so many other saints have in glory, namely, perfect fellowship with God Almighty.

Noah and the hope of comfort (5:25–32; 6:8)

When the genealogy comes to Lamech, descendant from Seth and Enoch, we hear this father breath out words of hope as he names his son Noah (meaning "rest"): "He will comfort us in the labor and painful toil of our hands caused by the ground the LORD has cursed" (5:29). The punishment of the LORD God given in Genesis 3:17–19 comes to mind. The ground was cursed, and man's toil and sweat would be needed to gain the food to live. But working cursed ground is painful, a daily reminder of our own sinfulness. Yet Noah himself cannot give us eternal rest.

Lamech sees the possibility that his son might provide relief. This indicates that in Seth's line of the covenant, people still lived in the hope of ultimate victory, a hope stimulated by the "mother promise" of Genesis 3:15. But the real need is much deeper than merely relief from hard and painful labor. Man's real problem is not bad working conditions; his real problem is sinful rebellion against Almighty God. Only God, through His Son, can solve this basic problem. There is no use in addressing the symptoms of the problem without getting at its root.

Marriage according to the "flesh" (6:1–4)

The opening verses of Genesis 6 have been the source of much debate and speculation. For example, who are these "sons of God," and who are the "daughters of men?" There are several views or lines of interpretation regarding the identity of the "sons of God:"

1. The earliest Jewish interpretation identifies them as angels, those spiritual beings created by God and who exist in heaven before the throne of God. Support is sought from passages such as Job 1:6; 2:1; and 38:7.
2. Jewish rabbis of the 2nd century A.D. advanced the proposal that the "sons of God" were tyrannical successors of Lamech (Gen. 4:19–24) or, perhaps, royalty or rulers.
3. The traditional Christian interpretation is that the "sons of God" are the descendants of Seth, through whom God's covenant line is continued.

As for the first view (the "sons of God" are angels), we must point out several things. First of all, angels do not marry! The Lord Jesus Christ makes this point in Matthew 22:30, Mark 12:25, and Luke 20:35–36. Secondly, what these "sons of God" do is seen as sinful, at least implicitly so in 6:2, in their taking the beautiful daughters of men as wives. If the angels are the sinful party, why then is the whole human race placed under judgment?

The angels should be the ones to receive punishment. Furthermore, Genesis 6:3 mentions that *man* is *flesh*, clearly keeping our attention drawn to the realm of human affairs.

The second possibility can be supported by reference to several Biblical passages such as Exodus 21:6; 22:8; I Samuel 2:25; and Psalm 82:1. In these passages rulers such as judges are called "gods." The reason for using such a word for human rulers is that they exercise authority and power in view of their office, functioning in a human calling as servants of God (cf. Rom. 13:1ff.). The problem with this understanding is that their children are never called "sons of God" or "children of the gods." Furthermore, was human society so separated into distinct social classes at this point in history? But even more telling is the point that intermarriage between royal sons and common daughters is not such a monstrous sin (if a sin at all!) that it would require the destruction of the entire human race.

The third suggestion probably has the most to commend it. Here "sons of God" refers to those who belong to the line of the covenant, apparently those people whose heritage is that of those who call upon the name of the LORD. The covenant line of people began to take increasing note of the beautiful daughters of men, the worldly society that was increasing more in numbers (6:1). The sense of the spiritual antithesis began to blur, and the "seed of the woman" lost sight of its distinctiveness. Just as King Solomon's foreign wives would later lead him spiritually astray, so too the children of God had their godliness diluted and then lost through intermarriage with unbelievers. Does not the same thing happen today?

God's patience wears thin (6:3, 5–7)

The LORD finally speaks in Genesis 6:3. The last time in the text God's words were heard was in Genesis 4:15, when

He tells Cain of divine vengeance against anyone who harms Cain. But now, when God speaks again, it is a statement of divine determination. The LORD has had it with the human race as we hear Him say, "My Spirit will not contend (or, remain) with man forever." When God created the world, His Spirit hovered over the surface of the watery deep. His Spirit gives life to all creatures, but when He withdraws His Spirit, man's weakness and frailty become readily apparent. The LORD's criticism of mankind is not that he is flesh as such. Rather, without God, man is merely flesh, i.e., weak, mortal, unable to sustain himself and live (cf. Isa. 31:3; Job 34:14–15).

Furthermore, the increasing number of people leads to a corresponding increase in sinfulness. Genesis 6:5 is one of the sharpest descriptions of how far mankind has fallen from the glory of God. While the "sons of God" *saw* the beautiful women of the world, the LORD *saw* "how great man's wickedness on the earth had become, and that every inclination of the thoughts of his heart was only evil all the time." Every thought, only evil, all the time! Before the Flood, there was no one who was righteous, no, not even one. Only Noah received the sovereign, divine grace to walk with God.

Seeing the rottenness of the human race, the LORD is genuinely grieved that He made man. Here is an example of where God is revealed in the manner of a human being, i.e., as one who has emotions. Since God knows all that He has planned in His wisdom, we cannot speak of God having regrets in the sense that He is disappointed about something that catches Him by surprise. That God is immutable and unchangeable in His eternal, covenantal purposes is taught in Malachi 3:6, Ephesians 1:11, and James 1:17. Hebrews 13:8 describes Jesus Christ as "the same yesterday and today and forever." But God is not a cold "Unmoved Mover." In the presence of obedience or in response to unfaithfulness, He responds appropriately with favor or wrath, with blessing or with cursing. He is not fickle in His responses, nor is He dispassionate with regard to our sin.

Yet God also gives man time to repent. When the Lord says that man's days will be 120 years, He is not saying that man's average life span would reduce to 120 years. Several patriarchs live longer than that. Rather, God is indicating the amount of time that would elapse before judgment of some kind would fall upon this corrupt race of people and the creation as well. How patient He is with sinners, even when He has set the date for judgment! This patience and mercy are evident in another ray of hope, the man Noah who, in contrast to his own generation of evil, "found favor in the eyes of the LORD" (6:8).

Points to ponder and discuss

1. Genesis 5 contains the constant refrain, "and he died." The Bible is the story of God's grace in Christ, but it also reminds us of our mortality and frailty. Read Psalm 49. How comfortable is our society with the reality, even the topic, of death? How comfortable are Christians with this reality?
2. We sometimes find the Biblical genealogies less than exciting, but the Bible never shies away from tracing ancestry and descent, especially of the covenant line. Were your parents Christian believers? How far back are you able to trace in your ancestry the presence of the Christian faith? When did the Gospel come to the nation of your ancestry?
3. The Bible does not record the age at death of the descendants of Cain (Gen. 4:17–18), but it does record the (long) ages of the descendants of Seth in Genesis 5. Why, do you think, might this be the case? What may

account for the great length of life of these early generations of people? Why do the ages of Biblical characters drop off in length after the Flood?

4. Enoch walked with God, while the Nephilim, mighty "men of renown," also lived on the earth. Enoch was a good man, while others were "great" men. Our lives are legacies to those around us but also to those who will come after us. What is the difference between goodness and greatness? Can a Christian be both good and great (in accomplishments, power, prestige)? Personally, what legacy (or reputation) do you want to leave behind when the Lord calls you from this life?
5. King Solomon had many wives, many of them from neighboring countries? Why did he do this? What does it mean to marry "only in the Lord"? What does the Bible say about marriage to unbelievers? Why does this happen as often as it does in Christian circles? See Numbers 25:1ff.; I Corinthians 7:14, 16.
6. What difference does it make in marrying a Christian outside of your particular church or denomination? Is this an indifferent thing, or is it very important?
7. Genesis 6:2 says that the "sons of God saw that the daughters of men were beautiful, and they married any of them they chose." What criteria or standards were the sons of God using to determine whom they married? What does the Bible teach about the importance of external appearance and the inner spirit (or person)? What is it that makes a Christian truly beautiful? See I Timothy 2:9, 10; I Peter 3:1–7.

Lesson 13

Saved Through the Water (Part One)

Read Genesis 5:28–6:22

In an earlier lesson (#1) we noted what appears to be a very deliberate structure to the book of Genesis, in that the text was divided by the phrase "These are the generations of..." or "This is the account of..." This phrase has already appeared at Genesis 2:4 and 5:1. We find it again at Genesis 6:9, "This is the account of Noah." At the end of the first "generation/account" section we came across what I called an "epilogue of shame." Genesis 4 traced the genealogy of the cold murderer Cain, a line that ends with boastful Lamech. Yet the Bible adds a small glimmer of light in the text when it tells us that Seth is born to Adam and Eve as a replacement for the murdered son Abel. "At that time men began to call upon the name of the LORD" (Gen. 4:26).

Two hearts... two purposes

The generation/account section that runs from Genesis 5:1 through 6:8 also ends with a brief epilogue of shame in Genesis 6:1–7. Spiritually the human race degenerates until we read this evaluation of the human race by the LORD in Genesis 6:5, "The LORD saw how great man's wickedness on the earth had become, and that every inclination of the thoughts of his heart was only evil all the time." The King of creation is genuinely grieved about this state of affairs throughout His creation-kingdom, and He resolves to destroy all living things from the face of the earth. Yet once again we encounter another glimmer of light in the text just before we move on to the next generation/account section. "But Noah found favor in the eyes of the LORD" (Gen. 6:8).

Man's heart is described as completely corrupted. Man's heart was headed in the wrong direction, always and in every way. This is an absolute depravity that must have made daily existence for people a great struggle. What was man's chief purpose in this sinful state? To glorify himself and enjoy himself as long as he can. Genesis 5 with its somber echo, "and he died," caused people to live with this purpose: eat, drink, and be merry, for tomorrow (or at least some day) we die.

But Genesis 6:6 tells us of God's heart. God's grief arises out of His holiness and zealous hatred of sin, but it also arises out of the fact that He beheld the creature made in His image, living in cross-purposes with His own will. His heart was "filled with pain." This is important to note because when we read of God's intention of destroying humanity in the flood, such awesome action is not done out of sadistic pleasure. God will have His justice satisfied, but He does not delight in the death of the wicked. "His heart was filled with pain." Even today our sins of bitterness, rage, anger, etc., continue to give the Holy Spirit grief (cf. Eph. 4:30).

Will Noah bring us comfort?

Often in the Biblical story we meet characters whose names are significant, either because of the circumstances of their birth, or because of their changed roles in redemptive-history (e.g., Abram becomes Abraham), or because the name is prophetic of something future. When Noah is born, his father Lamech speaks of his hope and faith that Noah will bring comfort (the name *Noah* sounds like a Hebrew word that means "comfort"). God had cursed the ground so that it would produce thorns and thistles. Work would go forward, but such labor would now be toil: difficult, painful, frustrating, and tiring. In the end mankind would still die and return to the dirt from which we are all made (cf. Gen. 3:17).

Living under God's solemn curse can never be easy. Rather, it is crushing. Man's pride may seek many devices to hide the reality of cursed living, and humanity may try to live in denial ("God would not punish us, in any case"). But to the godly (and apparently Noah's father Lamech still had some knowledge of a godly state of affairs), living under God's common judgment in everyday life is felt daily and in many situations. The godly know that only in reconciliation with this just King can there ever be comfort and rest from sin and its consequent painful toil. Just as Eve had exalted with hope in the birth of a man (her firstborn, Cain) with the help of the LORD, so Lamech finds a name for his son that speaks of humanity's hopes.

Despite the overwhelming predominance of sinfulness in the human race, yet one man stood out. Noah found favor in the eyes of the LORD. Like Enoch before him, Noah walked with God. That is to say, his daily patterns of life arose out of a desire to serve God and honor His will for life. His attitudes and behavior were in sharp contrast to the violence and moral degradation of his time. To be sure, Noah was also conceived and born in sin, as were his ancestors and the people of his day. He is not sinless in an absolute sense. But his heart knew the true and only God, and he brought his lifestyle into conformity with the heart of God, to the extent that God had made His will known. This is the result of God's grace, unmerited mercy. God's sovereign condescension in love to Noah creates a man whose life is righteous, a life that is like a star shining in the darkness (cf. Phil. 2:14–16).

Revealing the divine will

It is in this context of grace that creates a godly person, that Noah finds favor (grace) in God's sight. Thus God comes to Noah to reveal His intention and will regarding the earth. Later on the LORD would come to Abraham and would share with him His intentions of destroying wicked Sodom and Gomorrah. In Genesis 18:17 we read, "Then the LORD said, 'Shall I hide from Abraham what I am about to do?" God had already revealed prophetically that Abraham would receive the promised land and that he would become the father of a great nation. But Abraham also is made privy to the fate of the wicked, thereby prompting Abraham to begin a sustained intercession for the wicked city of Sodom. So too in Genesis 6 God shows Himself as friend and covenant partner to Noah (the word *covenant* comes up in verse 18).

In these two examples of Noah and Abraham we see a pattern on a small scale of something that is true on a larger scale. God gives the righteous greater insight and knowledge into the reality of things, including the things that are to come. During the period of the monarchy, God would do the same by speaking to His servants, the prophets. By providing us divine counsel God enables His chosen people to regain the prophetic role, a role that was lost in the sinful rebellion by Adam and Eve, but a role that is truly regained in union with Jesus Christ, our "chief Prophet and Teacher" (Heidelberg Catechism, Lord's Day 12).

This fact helps us to understand more clearly the events of Genesis 6 (indeed, to understand all the Bible!). For the Bible is not a morality tale of "good guys" versus "bad guys." It is a grand story of what God has done in Jesus Christ throughout redemptive history for the salvation of His elect and the redemption of His creation. Genesis 6 happens because of Jesus Christ, the descendant of righteous Noah. For the sake of the Christ who is to come,

God comes to Noah to give him revelation about the world-destroying flood and instructions concerning the ark in which Noah and his family will be saved from death.

Noah, heir of righteousness

Because Noah had received insight into God's intentions, he in turn began to build the ark. Hebrews 11:7 reads, "By faith Noah, when warned about things not yet seen, in holy fear built an ark to save his family. By his faith he condemned the world and became heir of the righteousness that comes by faith." I have heard or seen the following expression: "It wasn't raining when Noah built the ark." Faith is not a leap into the dark as such. It is rather trusting in things that are not seen, because of the trustworthiness of the One who speaks. Thus, if God says, "Leap into the dark, *and I will be there to catch you,*" then we can so leap, because we trust our heavenly Father.

Presumably it would be another 120 years from the time of God's announced decision to destroy the wicked human race and the beginning of the flood itself. Yet Noah believed God's Word, responding in "holy fear" by building the ark itself. We may well imagine that his efforts were alternately scorned and ridiculed by the society around him. Yet when God's people live in fear of God, then they need not fear man, either his ridicule or his scorn. Such faith in Noah's heart strengthen him with resolve to do what God had commanded.

Noah, preacher of righteousness

Not only did Noah believe by building in holy fear, he also began a campaign of *preaching* to the people of his generation. II Peter 2:5 says that God destroyed the world of ungodly people, but He "protected Noah, a preacher of righteousness, and seven others." Genesis itself does not tell us in what capacity or to what extent Noah "heralded" the message of God's impending judgment. Obviously his life was a testimony to God's righteous ways, and the building of the ark itself spoke great volumes to his generation concerning what lived in Noah's heart. But Peter suggests that Noah also spoke of these things. Yet we must sadly conclude that only his immediate family were persuaded. No one else followed Noah's message and manner of faith: they remained eating, drinking, marrying, and giving in marriage until the flood came and swept them all away. Only divine grace opens our hearts and the eyes of faith to believe what on the surface must seem incredible.

The ark: designed to preserve life

How often we may have picked up ideas of what Bible characters and physical objects are like from the Bible storybooks we read (or heard read as children), or from pictures in Sunday school material. If you ever have seen an artist's conception of what Noah's ark looked like, it often (not always) is portrayed as a huge boat with prow. It is more likely that the ark was built like a huge barge or a floating chest of enormous proportions. It was not a ship that was going sailing on the ocean, nor was it a boat that needed to be launched from a dock.

Another place in the Bible where the same word is used for a similar ark is the little floating chest in which the infant Moses was placed in Exodus 2. This little box was made of reeds lined with pitch in order to be watertight. It is interesting that two great figures in redemptive history, Noah and Moses, find themselves in floating barges (one enormous, the other quite small) to escape death.

The ark was a three-decked structure, a kind of layered floating platform, filled with rooms to house the human residents and the various male-female pairs from the animate non-human realms of God's creation-kingdom. Again, we could let our imagination run rampant about all the logistics of this (e.g., how much food had to be stored? how did these wild animals react to each other? etc.). But the Biblical text fails to satisfy our curiosity on these matters. The very fact that the animals and birds came in pairs demonstrates some extraordinary providence from God. Did God now also quiet or temporarily tame them for the duration of the flood? We are not told. It is likely that very young (and thus smallest?) representatives of each species came into the ark so that they might be the healthiest and longest to live "first parents" of their species after the flood. But even I should not let my speculations get too far from the text!

What is clear is that a male-female pair from all the animate species, beginning with believing Noah and his family, is to enter the ark to escape the great cataclysm of universal flooding. Just as the world of wicked humanity and the old creation with it are to die, so too in the ark a believer and his household with the (post-flood) "first parents" of the other animate species are to enter the ark to live. Genesis 6:20, 21 put it this way: the creatures will come to *Noah* "to be kept alive." He is the key figure in building the ark *and* storing up the right kinds and sufficient amounts of food for them. While God is in sovereign control of all things in the world, yet in a real and practical way, everything hinges on the obedience of righteous Noah. What a responsibility!

Noah, a type of Christ?

The above discussion suggests that in several ways Noah typifies Christ. When we speak of Biblical *types*, we are referring to those persons, events, and institutions of the Old Testament historical era that anticipate, or look forward to, the Person and work of the Lord Jesus Christ. One might say that Christ leaves an impression or an imprint of Himself in earlier moments of history. It is through the obedience of one Man, Christ, that we are saved (cf. Rom. 5:15ff.; I Cor 15:20–22). So it is with Noah and his obedience: his household (a congregation of only eight people!) and the rest of creation are saved from death in the flood. All creatures had to come to Noah, enter the ark and stay with Noah, and be fed by Noah.

Does this not picture the relationship of the Christian church—and every Christian personally—along with the creation itself, to Christ? "Without Me you can do nothing," says the Lord. "Apart from Me, you cannot live." In John 15:1ff. Christ reminds us that our life is drawn from the nourishment of the Vine that is Christ Himself. The world of Noah's day had become corrupt and rotten. Violence was prevalent in many places. Death reigned in men's hearts (cf. Eph. 2:1). But in Noah's time, that one righteous man became the narrow doorway through which the rest of history could flow and be rescued. In our day Christ Jesus is that narrow door, the only way back to the Father.

Covenant established

The Bible uses the actual word *covenant* for the first time in Genesis 6:18. But we should notice that the force of the phrase used in verse 18 ("But I will establish My covenant with you") is not such that covenant appears as something brand new, coming to Noah out of nowhere. A covenant is a relationship of life between God and His people, sovereignly initiated by Him but carried out in history with real human beings of His choice. Thus covenant (and that of grace!) is already presupposed and anticipated in the "mother promise" of Genesis 3:15: a Seed from the woman will arise in history to triumph in victory over the seed of the serpent. But to get from Eve to Christ, God creates a line of people with whom He lives in the manner of covenant, this relationship of merciful friendship and life.

Along the way of this history, God introduces various formalities of the covenant. But the point is this: even before the formalities of covenant are enacted along the road of redemptive history, God is seen again and again acting according to a covenant. So He speaks before the flood of securing ("establishing") the covenant in 6:18, but it is not until after the flood that God spells out what His covenant with Noah, his seed, and all creation will mean (we will look at this in a later lesson on Gen. 9:1–17).

Points to ponder and discuss

1. Psalm 2 describes the LORD's reaction to all attempts at sinful rebellion against His anointed one. First He laughs, and then He gets angry. Where else in the Bible do we read of God's "emotional state?" What does this reveal about God and His interaction with us in history? Does God laugh today at human sinfulness, or is He angry? How does Psalm 2 conclude as what is a wise response to the LORD and His Son?
2. Genesis 6:9 says that Noah was a "righteous man, blameless among the people of his time." Something similar is said of Job (Job 1:1). Read Psalm 18:20–24 and Psalm 26. In those two Psalms we note that the psalmist appeals to his "blameless life," and he claims that God rewarded him according to his righteousness. How do we understand such expressions, if all of us (even the Psalm writers) are sinners?

3. Eschatology is the teaching of the Bible on the *last things*. What are the "signs of the times," those things that will in history that signal the end of this age? Are some (or all) of these "signs of the time" occurring today? What things must happen before Christ comes back again? See Matthew 24; II Thessalonians 2:1–12; Belgic Confession, Article 37.
4. Will the human race become more and more corrupt before the end of history, or will it become gradually better as the Gospel message continues to go forward throughout the world? Support your answer with Scripture.
5. Psalm 147:19–20 says that the Lord has "revealed His word to Jacob, His laws and decrees to Israel. He has done this for no other nation; they do not know His laws. Praise the Lord!" God befriends the righteous and tells them things the world does not know on its own. God's people know about the good news of Jesus Christ, His Person and work, and they know about the coming judgment before God's holy throne. What is our responsibility to do with this knowledge? What does the Bible say about those who fail to make this known?

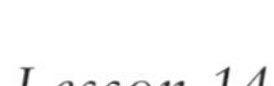

Lesson 14

Saved Through the Water (Part Two)

Read Genesis 7

Genesis 7 really cannot be separated from the material in Genesis 6 and what follows through Genesis 9:17. Therefore, we continue in this lesson to examine several aspects that emerge in the flood story. We are again impressed with the seriousness in attitude and action God demonstrates with regard to sin, but we are also humbled by the fact that He still was determined to bring to completion His grand plan of saving the world through the Seed, the Lord Jesus Christ.

Symbols of kinds and times

In Genesis 6:19–20 we read that all the animals and birds were to come to the ark in pairs, with the obvious reason being an anticipation of filling the world again after the flood. Genesis 7:2–3, 8 mentions an additional detail. Seven of every kind of clean animal and bird are also to come into the ark. The word *clean* in Scripture has reference to what is properly fit and prepared to appear before the Lord in worship. Only clean animals could be sacrificed to the Lord, and after the flood Noah was to sacrifice to the Lord in worship. It would be completely improper for him to offer a sacrifice of an unclean thing after the great flood! Furthermore, in Genesis 9 man is given permission to eat meat, but he may only eat the meat of clean animals, the blood properly drained. Again, it would be necessary that there be extra clean animals available for such a food supply. In Leviticus there would later be elaborate prescriptions given to God's people about what is clean and unclean before a holy, covenant God.

We also take note of several numbers that are significant, at least significant beyond this present story. After Noah and his family enter the ark, there are seven days before the flood begins. *Seven* takes us back to the weekly, sabbatical pattern of time, and it represents completion. In addition the rain lasts for 40 days and nights. In later redemptive history, Israel is in the wilderness for 40 years, thus out of the bondage of Egypt, but not yet in the promised land of Canaan. Our Lord Jesus was tempted in the wilderness for 40 days and nights at the outset of His ministry (an historical echo of Israel's probation in the wilderness). While we should be cautious not to press the significance of numbers whenever they might appear in the Biblical text, perhaps 40 comes to have the significance of representing a period of testing, of not yet being in the place of rest, the goal of our journey. An interesting fact: about 40 years after Jerusalem crucified our Lord, the city of Jerusalem is destroyed by the Romans (A.D. 70). Having received a period of probation, Jerusalem failed to accept her Messiah, so then God's judgment fell upon her.

The obedience of faith

Genesis 6 ended in verse 22 with a statement that is significant for us to understand what is happening in the flood narrative. Genesis 6:22 says, "Noah did everything just as God commanded him." Notice two things in this statement. First, it the LORD God who initiates everything in terms of announcing the destruction that is to come. Building the ark to escape the flood is not Noah's idea. The rescue is divine in its conception. Secondly, the Biblical text tells here that Noah did what God commands him. Genesis 7:5, 9, 16 point this out as well.

The importance of this can be sensed if one were to read the flood stories that arose among ancient Mesopotamian peoples. In Mesopotamian myths there are many gods, usually arguing and fighting among themselves. The Babylonian *Gilgamesh Epic* tells us that the gods destroyed mankind because there was too much noise in the human race. If only we had been quieter! Furthermore, the "hero" in the pagan flood stories has his emotions and feelings described in vivid ways during his ordeal.

But the Biblical text is more sober in its telling. The flood story is not a romance; it is not a tale of high adventure. We do not know what Noah was thinking or feeling. He is silent in the narrative. Again, what Noah's wife and family may have been wondering during the many years of the ark's construction, we do not know. We may well speculate, but it remains just that: interesting speculation.

The repeated refrain concerning God's command and Noah's obedience must not be lost on us as well. When Hebrews 11 lists Noah as among those who "by faith" did tremendous things in redemptive history, we learn that faith is not merely knowledge of important Biblical teachings. Faith is not simply a lovely warmth in one's heart. It is not only an attitude toward God and His Word. A mature faith results in works of obedience. Faith takes hold of God's Word, but that faith then in turn begins to work in love (Gal. 5:6). Faith without works is dead (James 2:14ff.). Had Noah only thought that God's Word was true, but then never acted upon that kind of faith, it would have been a dead faith. And Noah and all his family would have been dead as well. Faith alone makes one right with God, but a true faith is never alone in the life of a true child of God.

One plus seven: eight souls saved

One characteristic of Biblical story telling is that of repetition: certain details are told twice, even three times.

One can still read scholarly literature that points to such instances of repetition in the Bible and concludes that this "proves" that the Biblical account is something of a "cut and paste" job of putting together elements from different stories and traditions. But such a theory cannot be proved, and it hardly is the case.

Such repetitions are done in the Biblical story to press significant points upon the readers. We have already noted the fact that Bible stresses God's commands being fulfilled through Noah's obedience. Furthermore, we read several times statements about God's intention to wipe out all living things because of wickedness. We also encounter mention of Noah's family in several places (see Gen. 5:32; 6:10, 18; 7:13; cf. 7:23). Here is demonstrated an important principle of how God deals with us in the practical matters of our redemption. He is pleased to deal with believers and their households. Noah is the righteous figure in the narrative. But God, in His infinite wisdom, is pleased to save his household with him. His three sons and their wives are sinners (consider what Ham does later in Genesis 9!). Yet all eight enter the ark to escape physical death in the flood.

Later in Genesis 17 God will apply this principle with Abraham. He is the great (Gentile!) believer, justified apart from the law (cf. Gen. 15:6). Yet he is to apply the binding sign of circumcision to himself and all his household. Genesis 17 notes three times how the covenant sign is administered even to the servants in his household who had been purchased with money. Thus the covenant of grace *in the Old Testament* was never merely a biological, national matter. From the beginning the covenant of grace was open to all kinds of people, although it was administered through believers and their households. How important it is throughout Biblical history to attach oneself to the righteous ones of God, to their households, to their cities, to their nation. For example, when Lot began to move away from Abram, he put himself on the road to Sodom, a doomed city.

"Water, water everywhere"

The description of how the flood is brought upon the earth is clearly an echo from Genesis 1, but here in Genesis 7 we witness a reversal of the creation's structuring. Genesis 1 tells us that God created a firmament that is "inserted," one might say, into the cosmic waters in order to separate the waters above from the waters below. With the creation's firmament in place, life on earth could go forward upon ground that was dry.

The water that flooded the whole world in Genesis 7 came from two directions: rain coming down through the floodgates of heaven (7:4, 11, 12) but also from the springs of the great deep (7:11). The rain lasted 40 days and nights, and enough water was present to flood the earth for many more days and weeks to come. With water coming from above and from below, we have in effect an undoing of the creation. The sinfulness of mankind brings judgment, and that means not only death for the sinner, but the undoing of the creation as well. What is more, creation always does the bidding of the LORD, and it serves as the ready instrument to bring the waters of death upon the whole earth.

There are those who advocate the idea that the flood described in Genesis 7–8 was only a local flood, that it was not a universal flood. They point to geological evidence. Careful study of geological material is valuable and necessary. How its findings always "fit" with Biblical revelation, is a challenge, it is agreed. Christians must be ready to face the hard questions, even those raised in careful study of this creation.

Yet it is very hard to deny the fact that the Biblical material in Genesis 7 points out that the flood was universal and not merely a local flood. Consider the following things in the text: water coming from above and from below for 40 days and nights is an incredible amount of water (v. 18, the "waters rose and increased greatly on the earth"). Verse 19 says that "all the high mountains under the entire heavens were covered." While we do not know the precise elevations of pre-flood mountain ranges, yet it is clear that if the highest mountain is covered enough to allow the ark to float above it at the height of the flood, then all the mountains were covered with water. That is a universal flood! Furthermore, Genesis 7 points out that all life perished in the flood. "Every living thing... perished... Everything on dry land that had the breath of life... died. Every living thing... was wiped out" (vs. 21–23). The concluding statement of verse 23 is very sobering: "Only Noah was left, and those with him in the ark." Imagine floating for weeks on an ocean, no shore in sight, you and seven others being the only human beings in the world!

We learn here that God was just as serious and earnest in His dealings with sin and sinners as He was when Adam and Eve rebelled in the Garden of Eden. "The soul that sins shall die," says the Lord. God gave the human race a probationary period of 120 years (6:3). The sinful race could see Noah's preparations, and they could hear his warnings. But in the end even the patience of God can wear thin, and then judgment of a most severe kind becomes inevitable.

There is one more point to be made here. Genesis 7:16b, c reads, "as God had commanded Noah. Then the LORD shut him in." The two most important Old Testament names of our God are used here, but the usage brings out two important aspects of who He is. As the Deity (God), He has full authority and power to command our obedience. But when it comes time to enter the ark before the flood begins, it is as the faithful, covenant-keeping LORD that He is identified. He is both Almighty God and heavenly Father, *able* to do what is good for His believing children but also fully *willing* to do it for us (see Heidelberg Catechism, Lord's Day 9). The rest of Genesis 7 now proceeds with no more mentioning of God's names as the flood proceeds to destroy the world of sin.

Baptism now saves you

We have mentioned *typology* in an earlier discussion. To repeat what we have said: typology is a study of those people, events, and institutions of the Old Testament era that anticipate and point forward to the realities of the new covenant era in which the Christian church now lives. Peter makes explicit notice of this in I Peter 3:20–21. In the context Peter is speaking of Christ's suffering death for our sins, but then he makes some remarks that are slightly off the main thrust of his discussion. Admittedly, there is dispute about the meaning of the words, "but made alive by the Spirit, through whom also He went and preached to the spirits in prison who disobeyed long ago when God waited patiently in the days of Noah ..." (vs. 18–20). What is clear is that God was patient with mankind until the point when divine patience had run out.

But Peter continues in his tangential remarks. In the ark there were "only a few people, eight in all," saved through water. If the ark were the instrument of salvation for Noah and his family, then the water was the agent of destruction and deadly judgment. But Peter adds (v. 21), "and this water symbolizes baptism that now saves you also—not the removal of dirt from the body but the pledge of a good conscience toward God. It saves you by the resurrection of Jesus Christ ..."

How often do we consider the fact that baptismal water is symbolic of both grace and judgment? Or is that the case? Consider the following: in the flood at the time of Noah, the water caused the death of the human race that was rotten and continually violent. It wiped the surface of the earth clean. The cataclysmic flood, one might say, flushed the creation of all that was filthy and unclean in the eyes of the LORD. But this now opened the way for the righteous to emerge from the ark in due time to live for the glory of God and to enjoy Him forever.

But note also this: the flood itself did not change the hearts of the eight people saved in the ark. So too baptismal water itself cannot regenerate the heart, nor can it effect the conversion of one's life. Baptism is a sacrament. As such, it is a holy sign and seal; it is not the thing itself (see Heidelberg Catechism, Lord's Day 25). It points to the saving work of Jesus Christ, which is why Peter has mentioned Christ's suffering for sins (3:18) and joins to it a reference to His resurrection (3:22). Good Friday and Easter morning's events are the moments when our second Adam, the true Comforter (Noah's name suggests *comfort*), accomplishes our salvation. Baptism points to these realities. But, remarkably, Peter tells us that the historical event of the flood points ahead to the symbol of baptism, the sacrament of our Christian identity and union with Christ.

The flood thus has two powerful realities: destruction and salvation. The work of Christ has two powerful realities: the destruction of sin and the sinner, but also the salvation of His elect by grace through faith. And thus baptism has two powerful indications lying in its background: the destruction of sin by the blood of Christ, and our salvation through that blood. If we who have been baptized should repudiate, despise, or neglect what baptism symbolizes, namely, Christ and His work, we can never rest our hope upon the ceremony of baptism. It is then as if we had left the ark and thrown ourselves into the floodwaters. Outside of the ark was death. Outside of Christ is death.

The symbolism of the ark also must not be overlooked.

It was with deliberate design that many Christian churches were built to suggest the ark. But again, just as we may not place our hope in the sacramental water as such, there is no salvation in "brick and mortar." Yet the people who gather around the Word of God as Christians, are constituted the community of faith by God's grace. Therefore, the Christian church confesses that outside of the church there is no salvation (cf. Belgic Confession, Art. 28). Seven people joined Noah in the ark and were saved "through water." Today people from every tongue, language, culture, and background join Christ and His church, receive Christian baptism, and they are saved by God's grace. "Believe in the Lord Jesus Christ, and you will be saved—you and your household" (Acts 16:31).

Points to ponder and discuss

1. Read Matthew 24:36–51. It says that in Noah's time people were "eating and drinking, marrying and giving in marriage" up until the day Noah entered the ark and the flood began. Such activities are not wrong in themselves (see I Cor. 10:31). What is the Lord Jesus warning us about in this passage? How well do Christians heed this warning? How much warning do we give to our society, our communities, our neighbors?
2. Noah believed what God said about the judgment through a devastating flood, and then he acted upon that faith. He built the ark when it was not raining. How is it possible for some Christians to profess faith but then never act upon it? Are we saved by good works? Are we saved apart from good works? What is the relationship of faith and good works in the Christian life? See Ephesians 2:8–10; Titus 2:14; Heidelberg Catechism, Lord's Days 24, 32, and 33; Belgic Confession, Art. 24.

3. What was God's purpose in the older covenant to make the elaborate distinctions of clean and unclean things, animals, birds, etc.? When were these distinctions removed? Why? What, if anything, does this distinction teach us today?
4. What does our society believe about the judgment of God upon human sin and rebellion? If you think that the common views about God's judgment are less than Biblical, what has led to society to think this way? How is the Christian church affected (if it is) by such thinking?
5. Christ's second coming will be at a moment that no one knows. Then the whole human race will be judged. But before the end of history, could (or would) God bring a sudden and very widespread judgment of catastrophe upon the human race? If so, why might He do so? How could He do so?
6. Baptism is a sign and seal of God's covenant of grace. It marks the recipient of the baptismal water with the Name of the Triune God (cf. Matt. 28:18–20). What does Christian baptism mean? How well do Christian people understand the meaning of baptism? How seriously do Christians take their own baptism? What is more important, baptism or making a profession of faith? Why? See Romans 6:1–4; I Corinthians 10:1ff.; Heidelberg Catechism, Lord's Days 26–27; Belgic Confession, Art. 34; Westminster Confession, Chap. 28; Westminster Shorter Catechism, Q/A 94–95; Westminster Larger Catechism, Q/A 165–167.

Lesson 15

Creation Preserved by Covenant (Part One)

Read Genesis 8

The closing verses of Genesis 7 describe in sobering words the extent of the flood and its deadly effects: all the earth was covered with water for 150 days so that all life died. "Only Noah was left and those who were with him in the ark" (7:23c). The population of the earth was radically reduced, and the circle of the church was a mere remnant of humanity, a humanity that had been wiped out by the floodwaters of death. Yet in His wrath, God remembers His mercy and preserves a remnant for His own glory.

"I will never forget you" (8:1)

The opening words of Genesis 8 might strike us initially with some surprise: "But God remembered Noah." Had God forgotten this righteous man, his family, and all the forms of life that were with him on the ark? In the text the last time we heard from the LORD was in Genesis 7:1–4, and the last mention of His actions was in 7:16. Then the text goes into the description of the flood without speaking of the Lord God explicitly.

But God did not forget Noah. The idea of forgetfulness suggests among humans the notion of our frailty, a mental lapse that we do not want to occur, but it often does. When life gets too busy and we become distracted with many things, we forget things both important and not so important. To forget is a flaw that belongs to us human beings in our fallen state.

God is not like that. The verb "to remember" is used on

other significant occasions in the Bible. When God destroyed Sodom and Gomorrah, He "remembered Abraham" (Gen. 19:29), and so He brought Lot out of the catastrophe. When Rachel was barren yet desirous of children, God listened to her prayers: "God remembered Rachel" (Gen. 30:22), and He enabled her to have a son. An important point of the LORD's remembrance occurs in Exodus 2:24–25, "God heard their groaning and He remembered His covenant with Abraham, with Isaac and with Jacob. So God looked on the Israelites and was concerned about them." The very next chapter (Exod. 3) recounts the call of Moses in the wilderness to go and deliver God's people out of slavery.

Thus for God to remember is for Him to bring to special consideration His promises to His people in moments when they are in need. His thoughts towards us are in anticipation of Him taking the kinds of actions that will meet our need and bring deliverance. Noah is in the ark, and the flood has accomplished the purpose of divine judgment. Now God thinks about the next step of saving Noah by undoing the flood.

Creation re-emerging (8:2ff.)

When the flood destroyed the world, we noted in a previous lesson that the firmament was "undone" in the sense that the waters above came down through forty days and nights of rain while the waters below came up through the springs of the earth. Thus God brought about the deluge on the earth. But now God takes steps that restores the creation to a status of habitability. There are several parallels (or literary "echoes") to Genesis 1–2 in this chapter. Notice the following:

Genesis 1	Genesis 8
The Spirit hovers over the deep (1:2).	A divine wind blows over the floodwaters (8:1).
The water above and the water below are separated by a firmament (1:7).	The springs are stopped and the heavenly flood-gates are closed (8:2).
The waters are gathered together into seas (1:9).	The waters recede steadily from the earth (8:3a, 5).
Birds are created to occupy the sky (1:20).	Noah sends out a raven and a dove to search for dry land (8:6–12).
God blesses various creatures so that they may multiply and fill the earth (1:22).	God commands Noah to bring out the various creatures from the ark so that they can multiply on the earth (8:17).
God blesses humanity so that they may be fruitful and multiply and fill the earth (1:28a).	God blesses Noah and his sons so that they may fill the earth (9:1).
God assigns mankind to a kingly role in the creation-kingdom (1:28b).	God says that the fear of man will be upon all creatures (9:2).
God provides all vegetation for man's food (1:30).	God provides meat to supplement the vegetation diet of man (9:3).

All of this suggests that God has started over again with the creation, and Noah is cast into the role of a person like Adam. Genesis 1–2 portrays for us the original beginning of God's creation-kingdom, while Genesis 8–9 will show mankind and all creation with mankind in a kind of new beginning. Despite all the parallels between Adam and Noah, it is not really proper to say that Noah is a "second Adam," because that distinction properly belongs to Jesus Christ alone.

Genesis 8:13 says that the waters had dried up on the earth by "the first day of the first month of Noah's six hundred and first year." Truly this is a new beginning and a fresh (re-)start! But this restart after the flood is secured by God's covenant promise. In this way we must notice the very close relationship between the covenant of creation and now the covenant of grace in redemption. God's elect are the objects of His saving grace, but that grace always comes to man-in-God's-world. Christians are not saved *souls* to the exclusion of their *bodies* and the rest of the creation. The fresh restart is a new chapter for everything in the grand dramatic story of God's reclamation of His creation-kingdom through the Mediator, the true second Adam, Jesus Christ.

Enthroned over the flood

The reader of Scripture should not miss the several statements that make it clear that both the coming of the flood as well as the recession of the waters are completely orchestrated by God. The text builds up the story in terms of the coming inundation throughout Genesis 7 as God said would happen. Then the story reaches a genuine turning point in 8:1a ("God remembered Noah"), and afterward comes the reversal of all the story elements throughout Genesis 8 as God causes the waters to recede. Sometimes we speak today of "freak" disasters in the creation as "acts of

God." Insurance companies even use this as a category of description. But they are right in this sense: everything that happens in this world is under the plan and ultimate control of a sovereign God.

It is God who sends the *wind* that begins to drive back the waters and dry them up. The word in the original for wind is the same word for *Spirit/spirit* (cf. Gen. 1:2). It is God who directed Noah to build the ark, enter it with the various pairs of creatures, and now God again directs Noah's steps and all those with him out of the ark at the conclusion of the flood (Gen. 8:15ff.). God has directed and controlled both the destruction of the wicked and the preservation of believing Noah and all those with him. There are no "freak" occurrences in nature when there is a sovereign God that exists. Nothing happens by chance or through blind fate. God's hands control all that happens in this world (cf. Heidelberg Catechism, Lord's Day 10). God's throne is fixed in the heavens. Below Him was a mighty flood, but He sat unshaken in sovereign splendor over that flood. What a great King we have!

Worship in the creation-temple (8:20)

Noah emerges from the ark with the creation hosts of animals, birds, and the rest. But the first activity of man following the flood is an act of worship. The rest of life—its time and space—is sanctified by bringing it before the sovereign LORD in worship. The altar is a miniature mountain upon which the substitutes for the sinner are placed and there consumed by fire. Now it becomes very obvious why God directed Noah in his preparations to take aboard the ark enough of the clean animals and birds. They are now presented before God in worship to Him.

Genesis 8:20 tells us that these are sacrificed as burnt offerings. Leviticus 1 (also 6:8–13; 8:18–21; and 16:24) would later give the fuller description of what was involved in burnt offerings for the people of Israel. Admittedly, the elaborate prescriptions for the various offerings in early Leviticus are not "exciting" reading for most Christians. Yet here too there is something of our salvation spelled out in symbolic representation. The burnt offering was primarily a dedication offering, although making atonement for sin also belonged to its purposes. Normally one offered a flawless male animal (bull or ram) or a male bird (dove or pigeon) if one were poor. The sacrificial animal was completely consumed by the fire on that altar (although the valuable hides could be preserved; Lev. 7:8).

What did this all mean? Because God is so holy that He cannot even look upon sin, and yet we must appear before Him with the gifts of our service, sacrifice becomes absolutely necessary. The worshiper must be without blemish (no sins). Therefore, the animal without any defect represented the worshiper *as he should have been* (mankind as originally created). When the worshiper placed his hands on the animal (Lev. 1:3–4), he was identifying with the animal (his substitute), but now in such a way that the sins were symbolically transferred to the animal. The animal, originally "knowing no sin," now became sin and subject to its penalty, namely, death. The animal is then slaughtered, and its blood is shed.

By sacrificing burnt offerings in worship following the flood, Noah was declaring to God that he was a sinner saved only by God's grace and undeserved mercy. But more than that, Noah was saying that this burnt offering represented the total dedication of his life in service to God. Romans 12:1ff. says that very same thing to the Christian believer today. In the light of such marvelous mercy, we offer our very selves, body and soul, in living sacrifice to the Lord. That is part of our comfort—offering ourselves readily and willingly to a faithful Savior, body and soul, in life and in death.

Saved, yet sinners (8:21)

The LORD's reaction to the sacrifice of Noah is very positive. Our God does not need our worship, but as a covenant partner to His people, He does *want* it. God is pleased to enter into union and communion with those who trust Him and love Him. But it is not the smell of the burnt animal flesh that pleases Him, but it is the heart of the worshiper that draws His favorable response. Psalms 50 and 51 make this clear. In the pagan myths we read that the gods swarmed around the sacrifices of man like flies on dead meat. In Hinduism even today the pious Hindu will put out food and water in order to feed his demonic gods (after all, even gods have to eat!). But our God is never hungry, and if He were, He would not tell us (Ps. 50:12). Indeed, the cattle on a thousand hills are His (Ps. 50:10).

It is in connection with the sacrifice offered by this human mediator that the *Lord* makes the statement that He will never again curse the ground because of man. The *Lord* God had cursed the ground in Genesis 3:17 in His statement to the man following the disobedience in eating from the tree of the knowledge of good and evil. Initially we might think that this is the curse that is lifted here in Genesis 8:21. More likely, our interpretation must see the statement regarding no more curse to be in parallel with the other statement in verse 21: "never again will I destroy all living creatures, as I have done." In other words, God is saying that His wrath and curse will never be manifested again in the manner of a flood (as Genesis 9 will say in elaboration). There will be another judgment, but the next universal judgment will be with fire that will dissolve the created elements and purge away all sin (cf. II Peter 3:7, 10).

The Scripture's description of the Lord's reaction to Noah's sacrifice contains a truly striking statement. He promises never to curse the ground because of man, but then He adds, "Even though every inclination of his heart is evil from childhood."

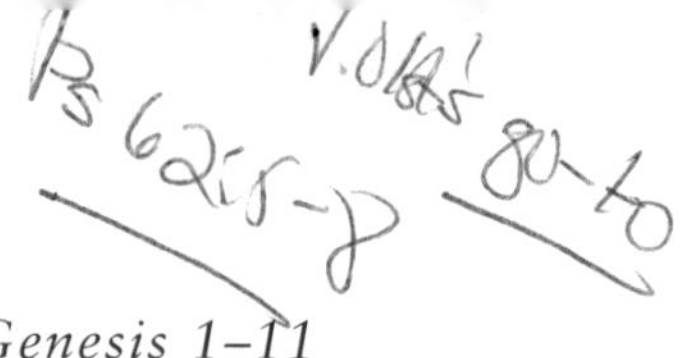

A similar statement occurs in Genesis 6:5 *before* God sent the flood. In fact, the earlier reference is made in a context that describes God seeing the tremendous wickedness of the human race, and then His great grief because of what had happened to the creature made in His image, namely, mankind. This painful reality of man, constantly inclined toward evil from his youth (actually, from conception itself; Ps. 51:3; cf. 58:3), explains the reason for God's holy judgment. His holy wrath against sin required judgment, in one form or another. If someone sins, someone is going to pay.

But now, after the flood, God evaluates man's heart as being still sinful, every thought throughout his lifetime. Therefore, we might well ask, "What then was gained by the flood? What really has changed, if Noah and his family are still sinful? Was it actually necessary to kill the vast majority of the human race—admittedly sinful—if the ones saved in the ark are no better?" The thoughtful reader has to wonder from time to time in reading the story of God's dealings with His own people (to say nothing about His patience with the whole world), namely, "Why does God even bother?" Why, indeed?

We are almost faced with a paradox here: man continues to be a sinner from his childhood. Yet in the face of sacrifice and worship by the righteous, God holds back that universal fire judgment until the end of all time, and He certainly will never again destroy the whole world with a flood. Even the righteous are sinners (as Genesis 9 will clearly show), yet God's grace and salvation are revealed to them. The God of Noah is patient and longsuffering, abounding in mercy. That God is the Father of the Lord Jesus Christ, and because of Christ, He is our Father. "Why does God bother?" It is because of Jesus Christ, His vicarious death and resurrection for us. The covenant of grace again emerges before us in this story.

Seasons fixed by wisdom divine (8:22)

God's mercy is not only shown to sinners who come to Him through worship and sacrifice, but God's mercy now establishes the creation and all its diversities of working and functioning. Genesis 8:22 mentions the various opposites that we experience in time, both on a daily basis but also on a yearly basis. The regular cycles of time move us through a day's routine, then added together, they bring us through each passing year. Consider what this means for this promise of God to be true. The spinning of the earth on its axis must continue—under divine power and wisdom. Then this planet must move through an orbit around the sun, neither spinning out of control nor hurtling into the sun. The time of planting presupposes that we have fields for planting and the seed to put into the ground. To gather a harvest means that the Lord has sent sufficient rainfall and enough sunshine and warmth to allow the crops to grow. In this way God's word of providence and daily care shows His Fatherly goodness to all creatures. Psalm 145:9 rings true for God's saints, "The LORD is good to all; He has compassion on all He has made."

Points to ponder and discuss

1. Read Psalm 42:9, Psalm 77:9, and Isaiah 49:14. Can the LORD ever forget His own people? Yet why do believers from time to time feel that they have been forgotten? What are such moments like in a Christian's life? What causes these periods in our Christian experience, often described in the Psalms? What is a Biblical understanding of such experiences in which it seems that God has forgotten us?
2. In 1993 there was severe flooding throughout much of the central areas of North America. Many people sought

scientific causes for the rain and flooding, while many others would not talk about God being behind the weather phenomena of that year. Why not? What role do scientific reasons have in our discussion of these weather events (or earthquakes, droughts, etc.)? Does God speak to us in these events? If so, how can we discern what He wants us to hear? See Heidelberg Catechism, Lord's Day 10.

3. Those who died in the flood were sinful. But Noah and his family are also sinful. Is God being fair to save some while condemning others to hell, when the whole human race is sinful? What should our perspective be with regard to God's grace and His justice? What do we say to those who accuse God of being unjust?
4. Read Romans 12. For Noah, surviving the great flood was a spectacular thing. Worship and dedication to God followed that salvation. Why is that so? What is the relationship (or, the connection) between salvation (grace) and service (gratitude)? How vigorous are Christians in their service to the Lord as described in Romans 12? What can we do to encourage (or stimulate) each other to love and good works (cf. Luke 7:47; Heb. 10:24, 25)?
5. God is a God of order and not disorder (cf. I Cor. 14:33, 40). This allows for the study of science and various laws in the natural order. Two plus two equals four, is a fact that is "true" for the Christian and the non-Christian alike. How does a Christian and a non-Christian approach this reality, that there are laws and observable patterns in the world around us? Does this strengthen or weaken the cause of Christian education and instruction?
6. Romans 1:18ff. says that all people know God exists from what they see and experience in the world. What does it mean that people are without excuse? Do we need to "prove" God's existence to unbelievers? Is it possible to prove God exists?

Lesson 16

Creation Preserved by Covenant (Part Two)

Read Genesis 9:1–17

There is much in this passage that builds upon what is said in Genesis 8, especially 8:21, 22. Genesis 9:1–17 elaborates on the blessing of God upon the whole of His creation-kingdom, particularly upon the race that would arise from Noah and his three sons. The passage under our consideration in this lesson is nicely divided into two portions: 9:1–7 and 9:8–17. In the first section verse 1 and verse 7 both record God's statement of blessing, particularly in terms of fruitfulness and increase in numbers. Genesis 9:1 and 9:8 both note God's speech to Noah (thus marking opening sections). Finally, 9:9 and 9:17 both mention God's establishment of His covenant. In this way the reader notes the concerns of the passages under study.

Blessing for dominion—again (9:1–3, 7)

In the previous lesson we noted several of God's actions in restoring the world to livable conditions after the flood, actions that parallel what He did during the creation week. Especially noteworthy are the statements of blessing given to mankind in Genesis 1:28 and now again in Genesis 9:1–3. The slight differences in the wording need not keep us from seeing the principal point: mankind was created to serve in office before God, working as prophet, priest, and king in His creation-kingdom. For that end we were created in God's holy and divine image, with righteousness, holiness, and true knowledge of God.

God pronounced a benediction (blessing) upon mankind in the beginning so that there might be an increase in number, to fill the earth, to rule and subdue it. Here again comes the divine blessing. Before the rebellion of our first parents, there was perfect harmony throughout creation, a peaceable atmosphere that had the animals and birds under man but not afraid of man. Sin has changed all this in a very radical way. So God instills "fear and dread" of human beings into the animals and birds of the creation. This points out the hierarchy, so to speak, that a God-ordained creation contains. Mankind is over the rest of creation, even in his fallen, sinful state. God says, "They are given into your hands" (9:3c).

The repetition of the dominion mandate takes away from Christians all excuses that might be raised to keep us from active involvement in the full range of living in this creation and in every legitimate area of human society. If one were to say that God is speaking here about agricultural pursuits alone, the immediate response is to point out that even there, agriculture today necessitates the following: machinery necessary for productive labor, economic planning, proper land use policies and practices, division of labor, good national infrastructure (roads, rails, etc.), and so much more. God did not cleanse the world physically of sinners and then bless the family of righteous Noah in order for them to hide their light under a bushel nor to retreat to the comfort zones of the creation. Divine benediction is for worldwide dominion.

Life is in the blood (9:4–6)

God now in the post-flood situation allows mankind to eat meat. Apparently the human body always could accommodate the consummation of meat, but in the beginning God had restricted the human diet to the earth's vegetation. Yet even now He places some restrictions upon the eating of meat. This parallels the diet statements of Genesis 1–2. All plant life was available to our first parents, but not that of the tree of the knowledge of good and evil. Now, all is available for man to eat, but not the blood of the animal. The blood must be separated from the meat so that the blood is not consumed. Why is this the case?

We should not think of the blood as containing a ghost or spirit. The Bible must not be understood to teach a primitive kind of animism (the belief that everything has a spirit in it). Very simply, blood carries the important nutrients, sugars, oxygen, disease-fighting cells, etc., that all make physical life possible. When *blood* is separated from the flesh, death results. Blood is absolutely necessary for life, and life is a gift of God. That is why the shedding of blood is so central in the sacrificial system of the covenant (see Heb. 9:22b). The animal dies; its blood is shed on behalf of the worshiper. Blood thus comes to represent life, and life belongs to God. All of this points to Jesus Christ's sacrifice on the Cross for our forgiveness and cleansing from sin.

God so values human life, even in its sinful state, that He prescribes the death penalty for any human being and even for any animal (9:5b; Exod. 21:28–32) that takes a human life. The first sin recorded after the rebellion of our first parents was fratricide, that is, the murder of a brother. Cain was worthy of death, but God showed undeserved mercy on Cain when he "threw himself on the mercy of the (divine) court." No other creature—only man—is made in the image of God, and God reveals here again His desire to defend life by means of the severest penalty and sanctions. "Whoever sheds the blood of man, by man shall his blood be shed; for in the image of God has God made man" (9:6).

Later on in history the LORD God establishes the cities of refuge when any blood was shed in the land of Canaan (see Num. 35:6ff.). Even if the death were an accident, the avenger (i.e., the relative who pursued the killer) sought to require the life of the killer in order to maintain justice. We read in Numbers 35:33: "Do not pollute the land where you are. Bloodshed pollutes the land, and atonement cannot be made for the land on which blood has been shed, except by the blood of the one who shed it." If the death were accidental, the accused could stay in the safety of the city of refuge until the death of the high priest. But if the death were intentional, the killer was himself executed. God is very serious about this. Count how many times in Genesis 9:5 we read this phrase: "I will demand an accounting."

This informs us of a basic principle of human government: protection of life, innocent life, from everyone and from everything that would unjustly take life away. The principle of "life for life," spelled out even more in the laws of God for Israel, reveal to us that the LORD is profoundly "pro-life." We should note that this prohibition of murder is given many years before the laws come to us at Mt. Sinai. This law belongs to all mankind, not just to the people of God. Romans 13:1–7 reminds us that the servants who lead in government have a God-given task, one for which they must give an account someday.

All creatures great and small (9:8–11)

God created us to rule all things and have dominion over all creatures. This is both mankind's glory and responsibility. But all things suffer and groan when mankind falls into sin. Thus the creation also died in the flood while a remnant of the creation is brought through the flood and preserved with Noah. Together with righteous Noah, the animals, birds, and every other creature come forth from the ark to proliferate over the whole earth. These creatures remain under mankind's rule and dominion, fearful of man and defensive, occasionally showing the effects of sin in this world when they take human life. Yet they benefit from God's grace as well.

Psalm 104 celebrates in worshipful song the regularities and the patterns that are interwoven throughout the whole of creation. The LORD "set the earth on its foundation; it can never be moved ... The birds of the air nest by the waters; they sing among the branches... The lions roar for their pray and seek their food from God" (Ps. 104:5, 12, 21). God takes care of the birds (Matt. 6:26). He dresses the lilies of the field with beauty that even outshines the splendor of Solomon (Matt. 6:28–30). When we pursue things in our high anxiety, then the creation groans because of us (Rom. 8:19ff.), but it rejoices at the prospect of the coming of the LORD (Ps. 96:11–13; 98:7–9).

A covenant promise, signed and sealed (9:12–16)

When God makes a covenant, He gives a sign to serve as a reminder to one or both of the parties of what is promised and obligated in the covenant. By the observance of this sign—either by seeing it or using it—the covenant is kept before the mind and heart of the covenant parties. The tree of life represented God's promise of everlasting life to those who obey Him. Later on, the sign of circumcision is the sign that God's people cannot live unless sinfulness is cut away (Gen. 17:11). The Sabbath is a sign that Israel is God's own people (Exod. 31:16–17). The bread and the cup of the Lord's Supper remind believers that they have life only by consuming Christ, i.e., by believing in Him, heart and soul (cf. John 6:35ff.).

The Noahic covenant also has a sign and a seal. God designates the rainbow as a perpetual reminder that He will never again destroy the world with a flood. If we may think of the flood as God's battle against the sinful world, a battle He has won, then after the battle He hangs up His battle bow (same word used for *rainbow*). Peace and prosperity can now follow. This is His sovereign promise, given to benefit not just the human race, but also all the earth (9:12–17). What is striking is that God puts the rainbow to this use, not merely for our comfort, but also as a reminder to Himself. Notice these words: "I will remember My covenant" (9:15) ... "Whenever the rainbow appears in the clouds, I will see it and remember the everlasting covenant" (9:16). It is not the case that God can ever become forgetful. But the text portrays God in such a way He has filled the road of redemptive history with those significant markers that hold our God to His covenant promises to His earth and especially to His covenant people.

Is this covenant of grace "common"?

There are those who speak of this passage in terms of "common grace." It is said that the whole of the human race and creation with mankind receives undeserved mercy (i.e., grace) from God in the covenant made with Noah, who serves as the mediator. But using terminology such as "common grace" is rather misleading and confusing. Grace, if defined as that undeserved mercy and saving power that God gives to His elect, is never common. Saving grace is given to, and made effectual, only in God's elect. But let us explain this further.

What God is doing here by establishing a covenant with Noah, his seed, and all of creation, does not serve as an end in itself. Read Jeremiah 31:31–37; 33:19–21, 25–26. These verses come in that portion of Jeremiah called his "book of consolation." Jeremiah did not always thunder judgment against God's people! In particular, Jeremiah 31:31–34 is the promise of the new covenant, one written upon the hearts of God's people and not upon stone tablets. In the new covenant there would be forgiveness secured through the death and resurrection of the Lord Jesus Christ. The covenant written upon the hearts of God's people is in essence the Mosaic covenant, the covenant that God gave when He brought them out of Egypt (Jer. 31:32) but which they broke (repeatedly, in fact, because of the wickedness of man's heart).

Jeremiah goes on to say that God's covenant with creation, specifically with day and night (representative of the whole creational order of things), holds and holds firm. If that were to be broken, then God would break His covenant with Israel, with David, and with the Levites. But the covenant with creation will hold secure until the end of time. The assurance that the believer has because of God's solemn covenant promise with His creation can be carried over into an assurance that God will fulfill all His electing, gracious purposes in Christ, the One for whom Israel, David, and the Levites were raised up in the first place. This is an important point.

In the second place, if God were to destroy the world again so soon after the flood, He would have every right to do so because of the wickedness of our hearts (Gen. 6:5; 8:21). But then Christ would not come, the elect would not come into existence, let alone come to saving faith and transformation of life by God's grace. To put it another way, if God destroys His creation-kingdom, then there is no history. If there is no history, then there is no stage for all the players of history to come upon and answer to their calling. This covenant secures the rest of history, both redemptive and non-redemptive. These two histories are not fully separate, although we may distinguish them.

After a destruction that is so devastating, the human race following Noah might well have wondered if God would ever do something like that again. After all, mankind continues to give ample evidence of wickedness! This is why God goes to such great lengths to say in His promises and to show in the sign of the rainbow that we need not live in fear ever again about a worldwide flood. The rest of God's dealings in history are even more clearly based along the lines of a covenant.

Noah in the service of Christ

But in making this promise regarding the creation, notice the effects: if God were to destroy the earth for all the sin that may arise, then the world would be under constant destruction. In order to save His elect people, those who are brought to saving faith, God will maintain the creation, its laws, patterns, structures, etc., even though the world in its present arrangement is under judgment, a judgment that will be executed at the end of time. This "covenant of preservation" therefore provides benefits felt by all, the righteous and the wicked alike. The elect and the reprobate experience many wonderful benefits of living in this world now. The Lord Jesus makes this explicit statement in the Sermon on the Mount: "He causes His sun to rise on the evil and the good, and sends rain on the righteous and the unrighteous" (Matt. 5:45). This is said in a larger context in which the Lord calls upon us to show love for our enemies. In this way we reflect in a greater way the nature of the God who has adopted us to be His children. The reprobate may not acknowledge the gracious Source of the sun and the rain, and thus they only compound their guilt. But God's nature is just and righteous, never demonic. He leaves abundant evidence in this world of the kind of wonderful God that He is. No excuses, O man!

God's ways are not always fully penetrated by our feeble understanding. But it is clear that this covenant with Noah and all creation is established so that the fullness of redemptive history may unfold. Noah exists both because of Jesus Christ and for the sake of the coming of Jesus Christ. In Jesus Christ all things cohere and hold together (Col. 1:17). Therefore, all within this vast creation-kingdom must submit to Him and yield their allegiance. In this light we may think of the covenant of preservation with Noah as truly gracious and wholly undeserved by us. Every day becomes a day filled with evidence of God's gracious covenantal favor to all His creatures. No more excuses (cf. Rom. 1:18ff.). May we never take this for granted!

Points to ponder and discuss

1. Noah, his three sons, and their wives were the only human beings in the post-flood situation. What tasks, practically speaking, did they face? How could they ever accomplish the various work projects? Can we even imagine what it was like to reconstruct human society after such a dramatic event as the flood?
2. Some religious groups (e.g., the Seventh-Day Adventists) do not permit their members to eat meat. Others prefer not to eat meat because it is wrong to kill animals, they say. Still others say that meat consumption is not healthy for us. What is the Christian's response to these various practices and their reasons?
3. Jehovah's Witnesses do not allow their members to receive blood transfusions from other people. The "soul" of the person is in the blood, they say. How would you respond to those who would refuse such medical procedures? Does the Bible allow Christians to receive blood transfusions?
4. Some appeal to Genesis 9:5, 6 in support of capital punishment by the state. Others say that the ethics of love in the New Testament require us to end capital punishment. How should Christians view this issue of capital punishment? If capital punishment is Biblically permissible, then for what crimes should it be implemented? Are there special circumstances where a criminal guilty of a capital offense could receive a different sentence?

5. Romans 13:1–7 assigns the sword (symbol of power to defend the good and punish evil) to the governing authorities. What happens in society when those authorities are no longer honest nor concerned about justice? What happens when government lacks the power or the resources to execute justice?
6. Read Colossians 1:15–20. Christ is the Mediator of creation and redemption. As the Redeemer and Savior, Christ's work is known and embraced by believers. But what do Christians understand about Christ as "Mediator of creation," or, "the Lord of all of life?" What should our thinking be in regard to "sacred" and "secular" areas of life? Is this even a valid distinction?
7. The teaching about *common grace* has occasioned sharp divisions among some Reformed believers, even leading to church splits in some instances. What do you understand this teaching to be? What elements are included and not included in this teaching? What better terminology can be used to avoid misunderstanding and even real errors in this area?

Lesson 17

Canaan and the Nations

Read Genesis 9:18–10:32

The genealogy ("generations/account") of Noah began in Genesis 6:9, and it now comes to its conclusion in Genesis 9:29. Genesis 10:1 begins a new section, one that deals with the three sons of Noah: Shem, Ham, and Japheth. Genesis 9:18–29 contains another of what I call an "epilogue of shame" that concludes the account of Noah. We have seen these epilogues earlier (e.g., Gen. 4). God's grace must move through a human history that sees a pitiful parade of characters whose hearts are constantly inclined toward evil, even from their youth upward.

Noah, tiller of the soil (9:18–20)

The text of the Bible begins a subtle shift away from Noah himself toward his three sons, who, with their wives, had survived the flood on the ark with Noah (vs. 18–19). Adam had three sons: one a murderer, one murdered, and one who became the hope of eventual restoration. Seth carried on the line of God's faithful. Noah, too, had three sons, but only one of them will carry on the promised seed. Through Shem we will see that God's blessing and covenant promises continue.

Following the flood Noah takes up a calling as a farmer, a tiller of the soil. This had been the work of Cain before him (Gen. 4). Let it be said that there was nothing inherently evil about such work. Indeed, God had told Adam in Genesis 2 to till the ground, work the soil, develop the world for the glory of God. All legitimate tasks and efforts, done out of true faith, according to God's law and for His glory, are good works (see Heidelberg Catechism, Q/A 91). Christians must rightly devote their talents and gifts to God in every area of life so that His honor and glory might be declared in the midst of our society. Although farming is a calling and vocation taken up by fewer people today in our Western world, yet it is one of many tasks where God may rightly be honored.

What Noah prepares is a vineyard, a grape arbor. Some scholars have suggested that ancient peoples believed that drinking of the fruit of the vine made one more fertile. They even suggest that this may have been, in part, why the daughters of Lot got their father drunk, not only to make him unaware of their incestuous plot, but also to make him more potent (Gen. 19:30–35). If this be true, then perhaps Noah also sought more virility in order to be "fruitful and multiply." But, if that indeed is the reason, what a lack of faith in God's promised covenant blessing!

Drunk and naked in his tent (9:21)

In this story we have the first mention of wine, the alcoholic drink made from grapes (among other things). The juice from grapes could not be refrigerated in the ancient Near East. Therefore, the bacteria that would be present in the jars and in the juice would soon begin to act upon the sugars within the juice to cause a natural fermentation and thus produce the resultant alcohol. To be sure, the alcohol content that would be naturally present in such grape juice would not be as high as modern day beers and wine. Nevertheless, if imbibed in sufficient quantities, ancient wine made one drunk. Noah drank from the fruit of his vineyard, and he became intoxicated. Wine "gladdens the heart of man" (Ps. 104:15a), but it also can make one drunk.

It is a well-known fact that people who are drunk lose several things, the most important being the ability to make quick judgments and reactions. They also lose some of their rational and critical faculties. They may think that they are capable of handling matters before them, but in fact they are impeded in judgment and movement. In Noah's case, he uncovered himself within his tent and lay naked. "Wine is a mocker and beer a brawler; whoever is led astray by them is not wise," says Proverbs 20:1.

Is this the same Noah we met earlier at the end of Genesis 5 and the beginning of chapter 6? There he was described as righteous and blameless, a man who walked with God and found favor in the eyes of the LORD. But we are reminded here that Biblical saints are of like passions and sinful natures similar to our own. Abram lied about Sarai his wife (Gen. 12:10ff.), and David committed both adultery and murder (II Sam. 11). Simon Peter boasted of his fierce loyalty and devotion to the Master, but before the cock crowed, this same disciple denied our Lord three times. The holiest of saints have but small beginnings in the obedience that God requires of us all.

It is interesting to note that the text at this point does not approve nor disapprove what Noah has done. To be sure, other portions of Scripture condemn drunkenness (see Hos. 7:5; Prov. 23:20–21; 23:29–30; 31:4–5; Rom. 13:13; Eph. 5:18a). As for nakedness, it has several kinds of meaning in the Bible. It was, in fact, our natural state in the beginning (Gen. 2:25). It is our state when we enter this life and when we leave it (Job 1:21a; Eccl. 5:15). It can be one's condition in poverty and want (Job 24:7, 10; Ezek. 18:16). Oftentimes, it represents being exposed, defenseless, guilty, and thus embarrassed and ashamed (cf. Gen. 3:7, 10, 11; Isa. 20:4). In other words, nakedness and sexuality are not always linked together in the Bible. Tragically, Western society has seen far too much exploitation of the human body for prurient interest. Sex sells in this society, and too many men and women are either exploiters or the ones exploited in the process.

The sin of Ham (9:22–24)

The exact nature of Ham's sin has provoked discussion among Bible students. The mere fact that he encountered his father while uncovered cannot be sinful in itself. Such encounters can happen, and there does not seem to have been any premeditation by Ham to invade his father's privacy in any inappropriate way. Later on, after Noah has recovered from his drunken stupor, he realized "what his youngest son had done to him" (v. 24). This last phrase has led some to think that Ham had engaged in some type of improper sexual activity with his drunken father. While such an interpretation is possible, the words used here do not require such an understanding.

Two things are certain. First of all, the fact that the other two sons, Shem and Japheth, cover up their father means that Ham did nothing to cover his father. He left him in this embarrassing and exposed condition. Second, that Ham told his two older brothers suggests that he was continuing the "exposure" by spreading the tale, thus subjecting his father to further dishonor and embarrassment. While Ham may have done something of a sexual nature that was sinful (the seventh commandment in view), it is clear that the fifth commandment has been violated. Children are to honor their father and their mother (Exod. 20:12). Ham sinned against his father by not covering him, thus leaving him exposed and spreading the tale within the family.

The other two sons of Noah act in stark contrast to Ham's behavior. So careful is their behavior that they walk into the tent backward with a garment or tunic to cover their father. They will not allow him to continue in a position of uncovered embarrassment. A spiritual division has become discernible within the household of this "new father" of the human race (cf. Adam's sons: Cain, Abel, and Seth).

The curse of Canaan (9:25)

In time Noah's body processed the alcohol, and eventually he came back to his normal senses. He then became aware of what Ham, his youngest son, had done to him (how Noah comes to know this, we are not told). Noah must have experienced revulsion and embarrassment that his son had sinned against him in this way. For the first time in the Biblical text, we readers hear Noah speak, and his speech is not one of blessing.

Noah pronounces a curse not upon his son Ham, but upon Ham's son, Canaan. Several questions have been raised concerning this. First, why does the son receive the punishment? Second, what was this curse? The reader has been set up along the way in the text to see the connection of Ham and Canaan. In Genesis 9:18 and 9:22 we read about "Ham, the father of Canaan." These are proleptic references (i.e., early mention of matters that become important later). In Genesis 10:6 read that Ham has at least four sons, Canaan likely being the youngest. But it is Canaan who is the object of his grandfather's curse.

The text does not tell us why Noah curses Canaan. Perhaps Noah is led by the Spirit to curse the one who is the ancestor of the wicked Canaanite peoples, conquered later by the Israelites under Joshua. Later Canaanites would become even more wicked than their ancestor (see Lev. 18:2ff.). Or, it may be that Canaan had joined his own father Ham in dishonoring the uncovered and drunken Noah. Some suggest that the "law of just retribution" puts the judgment against the sin of the youngest son of Noah (namely, Ham) upon the youngest son of Ham (namely, Canaan). At the same time, we should note that later prophetic words point out that each soul will be punished for its own sin (see Jer. 31:29; Ezek. 18:2). In any case, as Hamilton says (*The Book of Genesis, Chapters 1–17*, p. 325), "Canaan's father has eaten sour grapes and therefore

Canaan's teeth are set on edge." The sins of the fathers are visited in the lives of the children.

The blessing of the Lord (9:26–27)

Noah has more to say, but this time he speaks in blessing. In Genesis 9:26–27 he pronounces blessing, but surprisingly the blessing is directed to the LORD, the God of Shem. Evidently Noah saw in the actions of Shem and Japheth the working of God. By nature we hate our neighbors (including our parents!), but something of that evil and hatred is broken when the Holy Spirit regenerates us. This becomes a bright spot, one might say, in this "epilogue of shame." All is not black in the home of Noah, for the LORD has once again preserved for Himself a faithful and obedient remnant. Shem has acted in accordance with God's will. Therefore, "blessed be the LORD, the God of Shem!"

Something else to notice here is that the LORD through Noah is demonstrating His electing choice. Canaan is cursed, prophesied to become the lowest of slaves to the others. In the statements of blessing, it becomes evident that both Shem and Japheth are honored, but Shem will have pride of place. Japheth will have a wide territory (the name Japheth in the original language sounds like the verb "to extend"), but he also is said to dwell in the tents of Shem. In other words, God's greater favor will fall upon Shem. From Shem will come Abram, Israel, David, and thus the Lord Jesus Christ. God's sovereign grace discriminates in its blessing.

Noah lives 50 years short of a full millennium, almost as long as Methuselah before him. But in accordance with the judgment of God upon our old sinful nature, Noah died at age 950 years. Hebrews 11:7, 13ff., reminds us that Noah, despite his weaknesses and failings, lived by faith and died in faith, looking forward to a better city, a heavenly one that God

Himself is preparing for all those who long to see the coming again of the Lord Jesus Christ.

Noah's father Lamech had hoped that his son would bring comfort from the hard struggles of life (Gen. 5:29). Noah was a type of a greater One to come. Noah built the ark and saved a remnant of humanity along with the elements of creation, bringing them over from an old world to a cleansed (although not sinless) world. But then he succumbed to the fruit of the vine in foolishness. How urgent it is that God's covenant of grace keeping moving forward to bring onto history's stage the "Seed of the woman." He saves His own church, peoples from all nations, carries them through the judgment at the Cross, and someday He will drink anew the cup of life, the new wine, in His Father's kingdom (see Matt. 26:29; I. de Wolff, *Genesis: outlines*, p. 44).

Three sons: fathers of the world

Genesis 10 introduces another of the "generation/accounts" (cf. Gen. 2:4; 5:1; 6:9; 11:10; 11:27; etc.). The focus here is upon the races and peoples that descended from the three sons of Noah: Shem, Ham, and Japheth. The reader will notice that the Bible actually takes up the catalogue of nations in the reverse order of the usual order of the names. Therefore, Japheth comes first, but this will allow the family list of Shem, carrier of the "Seed of the woman," to be recorded last.

In looking over the vast numbers of names that are recorded in Genesis 10, we have to keep several things in mind. First, it has often been said that Japhethites are the Indo-European peoples, the Hamites are those peoples who live in Africa, and the Semites (from Shem) are Asiatic peoples. This is surely incorrect as a scientific description of population origins. For example, it has been said that God cursed Ham, and this is the origin of the black peoples. In fact, however, Canaan is cursed, and the Canaanites were not a black race. There is absolutely no evidence in Scripture that identifies having dark skin with God's judgment. Indeed, any biologist will tell you that the lighter skinned peoples descended from the darker skinned peoples (the darker gene is dominant; the lighter gene is recessive!). Any attempt to use Scripture to justify racial prejudice is wicked. Christians rightly condemn all attitudes and practices of hatred and prejudice against other human beings, created in the image of God.

Second, the list of peoples in Genesis 10 is not an exhaustive listing of every people group in the world. Many are not mentioned at all. In addition, amongst the names given here we will find individuals, places (e.g., Sidon, a Phoenician city perhaps named after an individual?), and whole populations (note the names that end in *–îm* or *–ites*; 10:4, the Kittim; 10:16, the Hittites).

Third, in general we can say that the descendants of Japheth are peoples who moved to the region of Anatolia (modern day Turkey), Greece, and to the north. They are the "Gentiles." The Hamitic peoples in general moved to the south and the southwest (northeast Africa and Arabia). The Semitic peoples moved to the south, the southeast, and the east.

Scholars count a total of 70 nations represented in the descendants of Noah's three sons: from Japheth, 14; from Ham, 30; and from Shem, 26. The number 70 seems to become a symbolic number that represents a total population (10 x 7 = 70; both 10 and 7 being symbolic numbers of wholeness). Later on, 70 people of Jacob's family will enter Egypt (cf. Gen. 46:27; Exod. 1:5). In any case, the chapter closes with a summarizing statement in 10:32, "From these the nations spread out over the earth after the flood." Yet in the face of all this diversity, Paul told the Athenians on Mars' Hill (and he says to us as well), "From one man He (God) made every nation of men, that they should inhabit the whole earth; and He determined the times set for them and the exact places where they should live" (Acts 17:26). Over all this diversity of people God has appointed Jesus Christ to be both present Lord and coming Judge.

Points to ponder and discuss

1. What does the Bible say about the use of alcoholic beverages? Does the principle of non-offense toward the "weaker brother" apply in the use of alcoholic beverages? Is it best never to drink alcoholic beverages at all, or is this too restrictive?
2. Is there a difference between drunkenness and alcoholism? If there is a difference, what is it exactly? What kind of approach should the Christian community take toward those afflicted with alcoholic addiction and drunkenness?
3. The Bible is neither prudish nor pornographic in dealing with the human body, including matters of sexuality. What kinds of things can Christian churches and Christian families do to develop healthy attitudes toward the human body (and sexuality)? How can we reclaim that part of God's creation that the evil one and the sinful world has taken, exploited, and perverted?
4. "Red and yellow, black and white, they are precious in His sight," goes the song. When we think of all the various peoples and cultures in the world today, do we typically think of the differences in the human race, or do we think of the things that are common to humanity?
5. We are all descended from one pair of parents, first Adam and Eve, and then later, from Noah and his wife. Yet in human history there have been those who have said that one race is truly human while another race is

subhuman or non-human. Is division along racial lines a "natural" thing, or is it a sinful thing? What exactly is racism?

6. God left the nations behind, so to speak, when He turned His attention to Abram and his call out of Ur. Yet He continued to control the times and places of all nations on earth (cf. Acts 17:26–27) for the sake of Christ. To the Romans Paul writes, "Is God the God of the Jews only? Is He not the God of Gentiles too? Yes, of Gentiles too, since there is only one God, who will justify the circumcised by faith and the uncircumcised through that same faith" (Rom. 3:29–30). What can you and your congregation do to bring the Gospel to your area, your neighbors, your community? How can you include in the church the variety of people living near you?

Lesson 18

Babel and Beyond

Read Genesis 11

After the flood there was only one family on earth. It reminds us of the situation in early Genesis after God expelled Adam and Eve from the Garden of Eden. But in the "generations/accounts" of Noah's three sons, this one family expands to many families. It becomes evident that God's blessing enables mankind to be fruitful, so that it might multiply, so that it might fill the earth. God's blessings come by His kindness so that we might live by faith and in obedience. But in Genesis 11:1–9 we encounter another "epilogue of shame" in the "generation/account" of Noah's three sons, Shem, Ham, and Japheth.

Textual arrangements

We should point out several things about how the text of Genesis 10 and 11 is arranged in order to see how Moses, under the guidance of the Holy Spirit, tells the reader this story. As we noted in Lesson 17, the genealogy ("generations/account") of Noah's three sons actually begins in Genesis 10 and continues through 11:9. Then in Genesis 11:10 begins the genealogy of Shem. It is in the account of the three sons that we read of the division of the world (see Gen. 10:25). Furthermore, Genesis 10:5, 20, 31, 32, tell us that the "table of nations" is given already presupposing the division that came about because God had confused the languages of mankind. Then comes the story of Babel in Genesis 11! Why is this the arrangement in the text?

Here again we see an example of telling the redemptive story in such a way that it does not always follow strict chronology. First, God seeks to point out how His blessing of fruitfulness in the covenant with Noah is fulfilled. Noah's three sons are the source of the nations of the whole world! But, then having shown this to the reader, the Holy Spirit then turns our attention to a story that reveals from where the divisions within humanity come. Then the text picks out one family, that of Shem, because from this particular son of Noah will come Abraham, Israel, David, and finally, the Lord Jesus Christ. In other words, Scripture gives us the "big picture," before zooming in for a redemptive close-up, one that continues the forward movement of the redemption story.

Unity in fear (11:1–4)

The number of people alive on the earth when chapter 11 opens is unknown to us, and that fact is, in the end, relatively unimportant. Whatever the population size was, the people that lived at that time still had a dominion mandate from the LORD to fill the whole earth, diversify their locations, and use all their God given talents for the glory of the divine Maker. But they did not do it. They were afraid. These people are terrified of stepping out in faith and obedience for God's glory. They devise a plan to stay together and build a giant city and tower, a human community, "so that we may make a name for ourselves and not be scattered over the face of the whole earth" (11:4). Two contradictory thoughts fill their hearts: fear and pride. They are frightened and intimidated by God's calling of service in His creation-kingdom, but they are emboldened to build the towering city of man. When man no longer fears God, he then fears everything else.

There are some faint echoes here of the fear of our first parents in the Garden of Eden in Genesis 3. When God came to them in the Garden, they hid from Him. They abandoned their service posts of caring for the Garden and guarding it. They did not want to face God because they were united in fear. Fear is a strange motive in how it brings people together against a common foe or danger, but it does not really unite them in a positive way. For example, during World War II, the Allied nations of Great Britain, the United States, and the Soviet Union stood together against the Axis powers of Germany and Japan, but the Allies were not really united to each other. Hardly had the hostilities of World War II ceased before the Cold War set in. At Babel, mankind is afraid—of obeying God. But that does not—it cannot—unite them positively.

The Babel builders remind the reader of a most powerful drive that characterizes many in history but also in today's world who wander away from faith in God's Word. Man is incurably religious; we all carry within us the "seed of religion." If the true God is not worshiped and obeyed, then a false god is given homage and honor. The creature is then deified. This false god (deity) can take on many forms, of course, because there are many creatures in this world. But a most convenient god is humanity itself. "I am the Master of my fate; I am the Captain of my soul," boasts the person who, in reality, knows not his own end.

Unity in pride (11:1–4)

A second motive for building this monument to human's ability is that these people wanted to make a name for themselves (11:4). The original language suggests something of a play on words and names. Genesis 10:31 noted the end of the genealogy of Shem as part of the account of all three sons of Noah. In the Biblical text this is just before the Babel story. The name *Shem* means "name"! Then following the Babel account there is the account ("generation") of Shem given special attention in the Bible (11:10ff.). Surrounding the Bible story of Babel are the lists of Shem, the man whose name is "name." But the Babel community wants to make a *name* for themselves!

This expression, "to make a name for themselves," is another way of saying how they want to create their own reputation and decide for themselves how they are to live. Man seeks to control his own destiny. This is humanism, bold and brazen. To bestow a name is often suggestive of exercising dominion and leadership. For example, in Genesis 2 man names (studies and classifies) the animals of God's creation-kingdom. Furthermore, God is the great name-giver when He creates man (*Adam* in the original language). Before the Lord Jesus Christ left this world, He commanded us to exercise redemptive dominion among all the nations of the world by making them all disciples of the Triune God. This includes teaching all nations to obey everything God has commanded and by baptizing them *into the Name of the Father, the Son, and the Holy Spirit*. In other words, in redemption God defines who we are by giving us His Triune Name. In redemption we are now named "Christians."

Since God alone is the One who bestows to us our name (identity, reputation), it becomes clear that the Babel project is an open, not-so-subtle rejection of God and His Lordship. The fear and pride of Cain and his descendant Lamech have now multiplied to characterize the whole of mankind. Cain had stopped his wandering to build a city (Gen. 4:17), and Lamech had boasted of his greatness in how much vengeance he was entitled to (Gen. 4:23–24). There is a real danger of a pre-flood situation arising again. Depravity again bears poisonous fruits in the descendants of Noah and his sons.

Divine investigation of the Babel project (9:5–7)

The central statement of this whole story (11:1–9) actually comes in verse 5 when we read of what the LORD's actions are. The Bible again speaks anthropomorphically (i.e., in the manner of a man) when it says that "the LORD came down to see the city and the tower that the were building." Here is a divine investigation, and now everything will turn around. The LORD comes down to see man try to come up to heaven.

In the divine statement of evaluation of what is happening God knows that disaster is impending if this proud project of fear is not stopped. Mankind will continue to amass power, and he will stop at nothing in doing whatever his heart imagines. Genesis 11:6 reminds us of God's words of anxiety and concern at the end of Genesis 3. The picture also recalls Genesis 6:1ff., the wicked situation that became the reason for the judgment of the flood. To destroy the world through a flood now would violate God's covenant word, but to do nothing is also out of the question here. God's wisdom shows itself greater than all the proud boasts of sinful man. He confuses their language, and thus He shatters the factor that helped to unite them.

Confusion, then dispersion (9:8–9)

If people cannot understand each other's speech, they cannot work together. The confusion of language stopped the Babel project. The original language contains another play on words. The word *Babel* means "gate of god" or "gateway to a god." But the word for *confusion* sounds like Babel (think of the English word "babble"). Since they could not work together, they began to move away from each other until they dispersed across the earth.

The Bible says twice in 9:8–9, "The LORD scattered them over the face of the whole earth." This is in reality an act of grace. God's sovereign action is to shut the human gateway to heaven so that the divine gateway may be opened up in God's timing and in His own way. Mankind has no right to storm heaven on his terms. Mankind has no right to shortcut the dominion mandate nor abandon the call to crush the serpent's head.

Jesus' words in John 14:6 (cf. Acts 4:12) are so very significant in the light of what God did at Babel. Jesus Christ is the Way, the Truth, and the Life. No one comes back to our Heavenly Father except through Him. He is the Door to the sheepfold. God's judgment against the proud cowards at Babel is thus for the Christ and the elect. His actions here are to continue to pave the road that will lead to Bethlehem and Calvary. Thus Genesis 11 is genuinely good news!

Pentecost: God's answer to Babel

At Babel mankind craved to be united and not scattered. They sought a name through their vigorous efforts to build a great society. But the LORD out of His rich mercy confused them in order to scatter them so that His designs to have mankind fill the earth might be achieved.

But this divine action, a judgment against humanity, should not lead us to conclude that God is uninterested in the unity of mankind. After the generation/account of Terah begins in Genesis 11:27, we will hear God call Abram and his barren wife Sarai out of Ur and then out of Haran to go to the land of God's special choice. This call to Abram would be to restore blessing to the creation-kingdom that had been lost to sin. Through Abram (and his seed) all nations would be blessed.

Matthew 1:1 tells us that Jesus Christ is the son of David, the son of Abraham. This is the opening notice of the Gospel record. But when the Gospel of Abraham ends, we hear the Lord directing the disciples (and thus the church) to go back into all nations and disciple them for the Lord Jesus Christ. This is made possible by the powerful action of the Holy Spirit of Jesus Christ (cf. Acts 1:8). On Pentecost morning that same Spirit is poured out on the assembled church, and the sermon of Peter that day exalted the Lord Jesus Christ (Acts 2). What is noteworthy is that

Jerusalem was filled with people from many lands of the Roman world. They heard the Gospel message being preached in their language. Though dispersed in homeland and different in tongue, they became united when the Lord Jesus Christ was lifted up in the preaching of the Gospel. On Pentecost there were 3000 people who then responded with faith and obedience, and they received the one baptism of the Christian church. Out of many nations, they were made one in Christ Jesus.

A new man, a new temple

Read Ephesians 2:11–22. In this exceedingly rich passage, Paul brings together both creation language and temple-building language as he describes the marvelous things that God is doing "now in Christ" (2:13). God dispersed the nations when they tried to unify on apostate, humanistic terms at Babel. But Christ, the second Adam, the new Man, is the blessing from Abraham given for all the nations of the world. Israel had such a rich heritage in God's Word (the "oracles") and the covenants of promise. With the first coming of Christ, the "far-away" people might be united with the commonwealth of Israel. Gentiles were barred (even physically!) in the past, but Christ has shattered that older Mosaic "dividing wall of hostility" (2:14). God's purpose in Christ was "to create in Himself one new man out of the two, thus making peace" (2:15).

Notice that Paul does not say that Christ creates two new men, one a physical seed and the other a spiritual seed. The creation language is such that the church may be described as "one new man." Gentile believers and Jewish believers are the several bricks and timbers that the divine Builder, the Holy Spirit, is bringing together, established on the foundation of the apostles and the prophets, Christ Jesus Himself as the chief cornerstone (2:20ff.). True unity is thus found today by submission to the Prince of Peace, Jesus

Christ. It cannot be found in the noblest intentions of international organizations, such as the United Nations. It cannot be based upon the lowest common denominator of so-called faith as attempted by falsely ecumenical organizations, such as the World Council of Churches. Christ and His kingdom are the true home of all believers, from every tribe, language, and culture in this world.

Shem to Terah: another ten generations (**11:10ff.**)

Bible readers may be puzzled why we take up the genealogy account of Shem here, if the text already spoke of Shem's descendants earlier (see 10:21–30). The differences in the purposes of the two lists may be noted. In the earlier passage, we see Shem revealed as one of Noah's sons who helped to repopulate the entire world. The Semitic peoples also constitute a major factor in the roll call of the nations. But in Genesis 11:10–26 the account has the purpose of showing us the covenant connections that move us to another man with three sons, namely, Terah (cf. Adam, Noah). This account almost certainly is a summary of the key figures in order to move the story line to Terah, the father of Abram, Nahor, and Haran. In the line of Shem, God maintained His covenant faithfulness, even though when His call came to Abram to leave home, that call came to people who worshiped other gods (see Josh. 24:2; Ur was a center of moon-worship).

With that call to Abram and his family, the Biblical story is going to take a narrative leave away from the nations. But that leave is not a permanent one. Before Abraham was, Jesus Christ is. With Jesus Christ, His Word and Spirit, God will go back to the nations. That covenant path back to the nations will be difficult. After all, Terah's son Abram has married a half-sister who is barren! But the God revealed in the text to this point is the God who is rich in mercy and who is able to call into being what is not. He pours out that mercy even today so that He might gather all His elect in from every nation on earth. In Christ—the Son of Abraham, of Shem, of Noah, of Seth, of Adam—the Son of God, we may again enjoy full union and communion with the living God. Just as it was in the beginning and someday will be fully restored again.

Points to ponder and discuss

1. What are the people involved in the Babel project afraid of? What really is fear, and what are its causes? Below the surface of our society today, what are younger people afraid of? What do older folks fear? The future? Finances? Health? Their family? What does the Bible say about our fears? See Matthew 6:25ff.; 28:20; Hebrews 13:5, 6; I Peter 5:6, 7.
2. What are the sources of a nation's unity? Common language? Common racial background? Subjection to common ideals, "traditional values"? Common respect for laws? Or what? What is meant by "civil religion"? Is it a danger, or not? How is it possible for Christians in the United States or in Canada (or any country for that matter) to be taken in by our national "civil religion"?
3. In what ways does our Western society show the kind of pride that rejects God's Word and His laws? What role do leaders (especially political ones) have in setting a tone and atmosphere that shows submission and reverence for the Lord? Or, is that not possible or proper in this day and age?
4. Using a Bible concordance or Bible dictionary, describe how the New Testament speaks of "Babylon." What is going to be the destiny of every "Babylon" that rises against God and His people? See Isaiah 13:1ff.; 14:3ff.; Revelation 18.

5. God stopped the Babel project dead in its tracks. In the Bible are there other instances of when God stopped people or nations in carrying out their intentions? Do you know of instances in the history of the church, or even in your own life, where God altered, or maybe even stopped, your plans? Looking back, are you able to see God's wisdom and His own plan more clearly? Why doesn't God always answer our prayers as we want, when we have tried to do something we think is obedient to His Word?
6. Read Romans 11. From the Semites come Israel and the Jewish people. Jesus told the Samaritan woman in John 4:22 that salvation is of the Jews (for from them came the Messiah and through them came the Old Testament Scriptures). Is there any special place today for the Jews (or national Israel) in God's redemptive plan? Or, are the Jewish people merely another nation on the face of the earth? What kind of approach must the church use to bring Jewish people to see that Jesus is the Messiah (the Christ), also for the Jewish people, in light of many centuries of persecution of Jews by so-called Christians?
7. In John 17 our Lord prayed for unity among His followers. What is the foundation for true Christian unity? How hard should Christians strive for true spiritual and confessional unity today with other believers? What is your church doing to build up unity in truth and in love?

Notes

Notes

Notes